ST. MICHAEL'S ABBEY LIBRARY

For the Life of the World

STUDIES AND TEXTS — NO. 2

Jerzy M. Domański, O.F.M. Conv.

FOR THE LIFE OF THE WORLD

Saint Maximilian and the Eucharist

Translated by Peter D. Fehlner, F.F.I.

ACADEMY OF THE IMMACULATE
LIBERTYVILLE, ILLINOIS

Title of Italian original:
Per la vita del mondo:
S. Massimiliano M. Kolbe e l'Eucaristia
© 1982 International Center of the MI
and Edizioni Cantagalli

Nihil Obstat: Fr. Mariusz Paczóski, O.F.M. Conv.
Minister Provincial
Warsaw, Poland 1987

Imprimatur: ✠ The Most Reverend Zbigniew Kraszewski
Auxiliary Bishop and Vicar General
Warsaw, Poland 1987

Given for the Polish edition: *Św. Maksymilian Wobec Eucharystii*, Niepokalanów: Wydawnictwo Ojców Franciszkanów, 1987

Cover art by Christopher Pelicano
Cover design by Jeanette Amestoy Flood

© 1993 Academy of the Immaculate, Libertyville, Illinois
All rights reserved
ISBN 0-9635345-1-3
Library of Congress catalogue number 93-72073
Printed in the United States of America

CONTENTS

WONDROUS EXCHANGE OF GIFTS	7
FOREWORD BY THE TRANSLATOR	9
PREFACE	19
CHRONOLOGICAL OUTLINE OF THE LIFE OF SAINT MAXIMILIAN	21
INTRODUCTION	29
I. SAINT MAXIMILIAN—PRIEST	31
The Priestly Program of Saint Maximilian 32	
The Priesthood of Father Kolbe in Practice 41	
A Life of Prayer and Sacrifice 52	
II. THE MASS IN THE LIFE OF THE SAINT	61
The Mass Register 63	
The Testimonials 82	
III. LOVE IN ADORATION	97
During Childhood 97	
At Lwów 100	
At Rome 103	
In Niepokalanów 107	
In Japan 112	
In the Concentration Camps 116	
IV. THE MILITIA OF THE IMMACULATE AND THE EUCHARIST	123
The Eucharist—God with Us 123	
Superabundant Font of Grace 128	
The Love of Love through the Immaculate 135	
The World: One Family through the Eucharist 146	
AFTERWORD	155
ABBREVIATIONS	157

Wondrous Exchange of Gifts

In the year of our Lord 1982, what gift do we offer?

What can we offer the Father of light and immortal King of the ages in the presence of the Mother of Christ?

This, dear brothers and sisters, will be our special gift, one at once characteristic of our times and sign of a saving link with the Cross of Christ: the inscription before long of the name of Blessed Maximilian Kolbe, victim of Oświęcim (Auschwitz), in the Catholic Church's roll of saints.

It is my conviction that this is the special gift all of us can offer Our Lady of Jasna Góra (Claremont, or the bright mountain) on the occasion of her sixth centenary. But is it not also true that this is much more her gift to us during this jubilee? Indeed, it is primarily the Mother of Jasna Góra who gives us this saint, nurtured in Poland and made perfect by his heroic sacrifice on the horrendous pyre on which his nation burned between 1939 and 1945.

Yes, it is the Mother of Jasna Góra who gives him. Was he not during life the special knight of the Immaculate? And did he not persevere, awesomely, to the bitter end faithful to his Lady, giving his life for a brother in the "bunker" of Oświęcim?

Hence, for the sixth centenary of Jasna Góra, we wish to bring this special gift, providentially prepared for the occasion. We wish to express ourselves in this gift—and we wish to realize in ourselves what our Blessed Maximilian says to us—what he says, so to speak, for us.

Here, then, is the point: his solidarity with another man to the utter limit; how, recalling the words of Christ: "Greater love than this no one has, that one lay down his life for his friends" (Jn 15:13), he volunteered to die in the place of that other man. The sacrifice of Maximilian at Oświęcim, in that place of horror and human degradation, is a challenge to our contemporaries, to the nations, and to society. He has become an eloquent sign for the times in which we live.

Today, at the feet of Our Lady of Jasna Góra, together with all the sons and daughters of Poland, together with all men of good will throughout the world, I beg that that sign be well pondered by all of us.

May the Mother's heart triumph!

May Our Lady of Jasna Góra triumph in us and through us. May she triumph above all through our afflictions and defeats. May she keep us from losing heart and from ceasing to battle for truth and justice, for the freedom and dignity of our lives. Do not the words of Mary "Do whatever He tells you" (Jn 2:5) suggest just this: that strength is made perfect in weakness, as the words of the apostle of the Gentiles (cf. 2 Cor 12:8) and the example of our countryman, Father Maximilian Kolbe, indicate?

From the Homily of His Holiness John Paul II
Feast of Our Lady of Jasna Góra, August 26, 1982

Foreword by the Translator

Peter D. Fehlner, F.F.I.

This book was first written and published in 1982 in homage to Saint Maximilian Kolbe, priest, on the occasion of his canonization (October 10, 1982). Its aim is to clarify and promote what is central in the spirituality of this Saint of the Immaculate—because it is so central to the love of the Immaculate herself—namely, the love of Him who is her Son, present in the Eucharist. It is this love that should also be central in the spirituality of every disciple of Christ, especially of those who are His priests and vicars. Consecration to the Immaculate has no other goal but to bring the child of Mary—and therefore of God—to share with them the love of her Son's love who died on the Cross for love of our love, a mystery prolonged for us in the Eucharist.

That love is essentially nothing else but an identification with the intentions of the great High Priest in consecrating Himself, in sacrificing Himself "for the life of the world". This is exactly what Saint Maximilian did in giving his life for another: he witnessed to the nature and purpose and everlasting efficacy of that love, greater than which no one can have. For precisely in order to love our neighbor perfectly unto eternity as Christ did on the Cross, one must first love God the Father and obey Him as did His Son, by being born of the Woman, the Virgin Mary, so as to die on the Cross. When a priest, ordained to celebrate the Eucharist, or when a believer baptized in order to receive the Eucharist, conducts and ends his life in just this way, the witness of his sanctity to the truth of the Cross is especially moving and efficacious.

How is such imitation possible? By total consecration to the Immaculate, by total identification of one's own will with hers, of one's own *fiat* with her *fiat*. And is it not also significant that Saint Maximilian is a son of the Poverello of Assisi, Saint Francis, who bore the marks of Christ's Passion in his living flesh as a sign of that perfect love of and conformity with the heart of the crucified Savior, formed in the womb of the Blessed Virgin? Does this not clarify the precise character of Saint Francis' profound love of the Virgin Mother, his Queen? That love, perfected in the observance of gospel poverty, consisted in total consecration to the Immaculate.

Such perfected love cannot but involve the child of the Immaculate Virgin in that struggle for the souls of men that has countersigned human history since the formation of Adam and Eve: the struggle between the Woman and her Seed (and His brothers) on the one hand and the serpent and his offspring on the other. This is how the consecration of the Immaculate to her Son and the very consecration of that Son as the Holy One of God (cf. Lk 1:35; Jn 6:70) are consummated in the victory of the Cross over the prince of this world. Thereby access to the tree of everlasting life, i.e., to the Eucharist, is made possible to the "rest of her offspring" (cf. Rev 12:17), the disciples of Jesus.

Another word for struggle is warfare. The warfare between the two militias is not political, economic, social, but spiritual; the warfare between two cities: that of God and of this world. It is a warfare over the possession of souls—by Christ the Savior through grace or by the prince of this world through sin. This is why eucharistic devotion, by its very being, involves us in the battle decided finally on the Cross, not only for ourselves but for everyone, above all, those most helpless or those most in need of His mercy. This is why, if our devotion is unconditional, it makes of us instruments in the hands of the Woman and her Seed for the life of the world.

Once it is understood that consecration to Christ is not possible objectively without consecration to the Immaculate, without being spiritually begotten of her, then it is clear how appropriate the name Militia of the Immaculate is for our association with our Blessed Savior in this glorious battle. This is why the concluding chapter of this study treats of the Militia of the Immaculate (abbreviated MI).

Since there is so intimate and unbreakable a link between consecration to the Immaculate and sharing in the sacrificial consecration of Jesus as victim on the Cross, it is only logical that our progress in perfection and our growth in holiness should be facilitated by our conscious and deliberate affirmation of the consecration to His Mother our dying Savior made of the Church and of every believer (cf. Jn 19:25–27) and which the present Vicar of Christ repeats wherever he visits.

Love of the Word Incarnate, and therefore of the Eucharist, is not genuine if not sacrificial. Such a love had the Immaculate Virgin throughout her life, nowhere more so than at the foot of the Cross, for the conversion and salvation of souls. Another word for sacrificial love of Jesus is chaste love. Love is chaste only as far as it is one with the purity of the immaculately conceived Virgin, the Immaculate Conception. Hence the link between consecration to the Immaculate and participation in the mystery of the Cross—the sacrifice for the life of the world—in the struggle for souls between the Woman and her Seed on the one hand and the serpent and his brood on the other.

How appropriate that the chaste, sacrificial love of Saint Maximilian, priest, should have been consummated on the vigil of the Feast of the Assumption in 1941. Such pure love brought him to the glory of heaven, acknowledged by the Church on earth. And though his body was reduced to ashes in a crematory at Auschwitz, it will nonetheless be raised and reunited to his soul on the day of Christ's return in glory to judge the living and the dead. That same guarantee is given to all who, believing and with chaste hearts, eat and drink the Body and Blood of the Savior. The reality, depth, and intensity of that faith and purity is directly proportionate to their devotion and consecration to the Immaculate.

In practical terms, consecration to the Immaculate and participation on her side in the war against the prince of this world means for the married a chaste love that honors the marriage covenant until the parting of death and that assigns, among the ends of marriage, primacy to the conception, birth, and education of children as members of God's city and as future citizens of heaven. Spousal love is truly genuine precisely to the extent that it is not sought or practiced as an end unto itself, but in view of sharing that love with the children conceived.

The love of religious, especially contemplatives absorbed totally in the life of prayer, is sacrificial to the extent that such love reflects the singular love of the Immaculate for the Savior by whose merits she was preserved from all taint of original sin, precisely in order to be the Mother of God and of the Church. Consecration of religious to the Immaculate, put positively after the manner of Saint Maximilian, means, by way of the vows, identity of their whole selves, in their wills, affections, and possessions, with the Immaculate, whose will and affections were perfectly one at every moment and juncture of her life with that of God in the love of the Savior and of those for whom He gave His life.

Finally, for the priest, sacrificial love can be summarized in one word: celibacy. It aims at reproducing in his life and ministry the celibate love of the High Priest consummated on the Cross. The celibate love of the Savior for His body the Church is an undivided, exclusive love for the Church, an extension of His love for His Immaculate Mother. The inner logic of the priesthood demands a love for the Church and the Virgin that is undivided, and thus celibate. That is why no priest can in practice be faithful to the demands of his vocation, and ultimately imitate in his own life what he does sacramentally at the altar, except to the degree that he is consecrated to the Immaculate, Mother of the Priest and of priests. For it was in her virginal womb at the Incarnation, by the power of the Holy Spirit, that the Son of God was anointed priest. Analogously, through her mediation at the imposition of the bishop's hands, every priest is anointed as such by the Holy Spirit.

One may wonder that so much attention in this study is given to the priesthood. This could hardly be avoided, since he who is being studied was a priest. Nonetheless, even if certain practical consequences of total consecration for a priest are more often touched upon, the relation of total consecration to eucharistic devotion for all is evident on every page.

How could this be otherwise? For in practice, where priests are deeply devoted to the Eucharist, there also the laity and religious will be. Where priests protest consecration to the Immaculate, there also the faith of believers in general will tend to grow weak or die. To take one recent example: effective dissent from *Humanae vitae* and from the truth of the mystery of chaste love it reiterates was articulated first by members of the clergy restless under the "yoke" of celibacy and then spread among the rest of the faithful. No renewal of the Church can succeed permanently, except that it have at its core the renewal of priests in the love of the Immaculate, so as to be more one in love with Christ the Priest in the Blessed Sacrament.

So, too, with the chapter devoted to the Militia founded by Saint Maximilian. His eucharistic devotion as the first fruit of his total consecration to the Immaculate could hardly have been illustrated concretely without abundant reference to the "pious union" he initiated to promote just that consecration for the sake of the conversion and sanctification of souls. It is not necessary to be a member of the Militia to save one's soul. Yet to the extent one grows in perfection and holiness, even without inscribing one's name in the registers of that Militia, one is implicitly involved more and more in a spiritual warfare. The MI was established in 1917 to serve as an effective, visible reminder of a reality fundamental to the security of our souls and crucial to our final salvation.

In publishing this study, the Academy of the Immaculate hopes that many, many more persons will in fact inscribe their names in the registers of the Militia of the Immaculate. But this book is neither primarily nor exclusively intended for members of the MI. Its publication is directed rather to all believers in the Son of God and Son of the Virgin: the baptized in general and priests in particular, to whom the Lord has entrusted the care of His sheep, and to all potential believers. It is meant to aid all in seeing clearly what is the source and heart of their life in the Church and how that life is to be quickened and renewed in them through the maternal mediation of the Immaculate and therefore through their response to that mediation: total consecration to her.

Surely the identification with Mary Immaculate, both by Saint Maximilian and before him by Saint

Francis, reflects and realizes in full the sentiments of a verse from an old Catholic hymn in honor of the eucharistic Christ and of His Virgin Mother: *Ave verum corpus natum de Maria Virgine* (Hail, real Body [of Christ] born of the Virgin Mary). If we strive to reproduce in ourselves Saint Maximilian's love for the Immaculate, surely we too, as our Holy Father says in the homily included in this book, will share in that wondrous exchange of gifts effected by the canonization of the Martyr of Charity.

The author of this book, Father Jerzy Domański, born in Poland in 1919, professed his vows in the Order of Friars Minor Conventual in 1938 at Niepokalanów, when Saint Maximilian was guardian (superior) there. Ordained a priest in 1943, two years after Saint Maximilian's martyrdom, Father Jerzy completed doctoral studies in theology after the Second World War. He has since served as editor of *Rycerz Niepokalanej*, guardian of Niepokalanów, international director of the Militia of the Immaculate in Rome, and simultaneously editor of the Rome-based quarterly *Miles Immaculatae* and currently is again editor of *Rycerz Niepokalanej*.

Well-known in Europe for his scholarly research and writing, he possesses an unrivaled knowledge of the life and thought of Saint Maximilian. Though simply and clearly written, so as to constitute an aid and a stimulus to others seeking to walk in the footsteps of Saint Maximilian under the guidance of the great Mother of God, this book is solidly grounded on original source material and reflects the depth and precision of the author's learning. It is the fruit of lifelong meditation by a scholar totally consecrated to the Immaculate.

This English translation is based on the author's original text written and first published in Italian in Rome in 1982 by the International Center of the MI and simultaneously in Siena by the Sanctuary of the Sacred Hosts (Edizioni Cantagalli) under the title *Per la vita del mondo: S. Massimiliano M. Kolbe e l'Eucaristia* and on the considerably revised text prepared for publication in Polish in 1984. To this has been added a chronological outline of the life of Saint Maximilian to aid the reader unacquainted with the details of his biography in situating references to these details in the text of this study.

For citations from the writings of Saint Maximilian and from the testimonials concerning his priestly character and eucharistic devotion, the system of capitalization followed in the originals, particularly for titles of our Lady and pronouns referring to her, though no longer common in English usage, has been retained in order to convey better the flavor of the original texts.

PREFACE

Guided by the Immaculate, to whom he was totally consecrated, Saint Maximilian Mary Kolbe dedicated his entire life, by every legitimate means at his disposal, to the salvation of souls. All his apostolic effort had a single objective, inspired by a single love: the will of the Immaculate One with that of her Son, the world's true salvation.

For this reason, then, perfect devotion to Mary coincides with adoring love for Christ really present, in His divinity and in His humanity, under the eucharistic species. To love Mary is the equivalent of loving and praising her Son, Jesus. Saint Maximilian's love for the Immaculate was in direct proportion to his love for his eucharistic Lord.

This study by Father Jerzy Domański, one of the world's foremost experts on the thought of Saint Maximilian, brings together in a single volume his eucharistic teaching, spirituality, and devotion and organizes this extensive material so as to stimulate reflection.

It would hardly have been a balanced presentation, indeed it would have been seriously defective, had there issued from these pages merely a portrait of the theologian and not that of the model for souls in love with the Eucharist. How many there are who knew

Saint Maximilian and still remember him on his knees in humble recollection before the tabernacle, finally rising after long hours bathed in supernatural light. And how many there are who still recall him at the altar celebrating Mass with inspiring devotion. Then, enraptured by the sacrificial mystery, he offered himself in union with the Divine Victim and in the company of the Immaculate, from whom he implored an era of peace. Father Domański indeed gives us Saint Maximilian, not simply the theologian, but the shining example for every priest and for every eucharistic soul.

The words of the title: *For the Life of the World*, first issuing from the heart of the Savior (cf. Jn 6:52), permeated this great servant of the Immaculate through and through and were lived by him unto that final, total self-immolation in the death bunker. If the world would not perish, it must for that very reason enter on the path, in fact consoling and gentle, of filial love for the Immaculate and for the Eucharist: the two loves that brought Saint Maximilian Mary Kolbe to eternal glory.

—Felix Rossetti, O.F.M. Conv.

Chronological Outline of the Life of Saint Maximilian

1894 *January 8:* Born in Zduńska Wola in Poland (in an area then occupied by Russia), his father being Julius Kolbe and his mother Marianna Dabrowska Kolbe. He is given the name Raymond in baptism.

1895 The family moves to Łódź.

1896 The family moves to Jutrzkowice.

1900 The Kolbes move finally to Pabianicé. Julius and Marianna are the parents of five children: Francis (the firstborn, known as Father Valerian while a Franciscan), Raymond (Saint Maximilian), Joseph (Father Alphonse as a Franciscan), Valentine, and Anthony (the last two dying in infancy).

1905 First Communion of Raymond Kolbe. Sometime before this, in the Church of Saint Matthew (parish of the Kolbe family in Pabianicé), probably at the altar of Our Lady of Victory, he has the vision of the two crowns, red and white (recounted by his mother after his death in 1941).

1907 Entry into the minor seminary of the Conventual Franciscans in Lwów in Poland (in an area then occupied by Austria).

1908 *July 9:* Vow of perpetual chastity by his parents.

1910 *September 4:* Investiture in the Franciscan habit and commencement of the novitiate in Lwów.

1911 *September 5:* Religious profession.

1912 On completion of his studies in humanities at Lwów, Saint Maximilian is transferred to Kraków to begin the study of philosophy.

October 30: Transfer to the International Seraphic College of the Friars Minor Conventual (Seraphicum), Rome, to study for doctorates in philosophy and theology.

1915 *November 22:* Completes doctorate in philosophy at Gregorian University, directed by the Jesuits.

1917 *October 16 (in the evening):* Foundation of the Militia of the Immaculate (abbreviated MI) by Saint Maximilian with six other confreres.

1918 *April 28:* Ordination to the priesthood at the Church of Sant'Andrea della Valle.

April 29: Celebration of his first Mass in the church of Sant'Andrea delle Fratte at the altar of the apparition of our Lady to Alphonse Ratisbonne in 1842.

1919 *July 22:* Completes doctorate in theology at the Seraphicum, directed by the Conventual Franciscans.

July 23–29: Returns to Poland. Assigned as teacher of philosophy, Scripture, and Church history in the Franciscan seminary in Kraków.

October 7: Initiation of the MI in Poland, including among its members priests, friars, and university professors.

1920 *August to April 1921:* First hospitalization at Zakopane sanitarium for tuberculosis.

1922 *January:* First issue of *Rycerz Niepokalanej* (Knight of the Immaculate).

October 20 to November 20, 1927: Stationed at Grodno, the saint assembles a group of lay brothers, and with the help of his brother, Father Alphonse, he edits, prints, and publishes *Rycerz Niepokalanej.*

1926 *September to April 1927:* Second hospitalization at Zakopane.

1927 *November 12:* First Mass celebrated by Father Maximilian at Niepokalanów (near Warsaw), a gift of Prince John Drucki Lubecki (*October 1*); transfer of the friars involved in MI work at Grodno to Niepokalanów.

December 7: Blessing and opening of new friary.

1930 *January 14 to February 4:* Journey to Rome, France (Lourdes and Lisieux), and Germany (acquisition of new printing presses).

February 26 to April 24: First voyage to Japan (by ship). Professor of philosophy in the diocesan seminary of Nagasaki and resident therein.

May 24: First issue of *Seibo no Kishi*.

After June 2: Resides in a rented house near the cathedral of Nagasaki.

June 12 to July 3: Trip to Poland by train through Siberia for the provincial chapter.

August 13 to 25: Returns to Japan by train through Siberia.

1931 *After May 16:* Resides at Mugenzai no Sono (Garden of the Immaculate).

1932 *May 29 to June 23:* Visit to India to found another City of the Immaculate (though not inaugurated during the saint's lifetime).

June 29 to July 24: Returns to Japan.

1933 *April 7 to May 30:* Journey to Poland by ship for provincial chapter.

August 31 to October 4: Returns to Japan by boat, with Father Cornelius Czupryk, former provincial and new guardian of Mugenzai no Sono.

1936 *May 23 to June 21:* Final departure from Japan and return to Poland by boat for the provincial chapter of 1936, where Father Maximilian is reappointed guardian of Niepokalanów.

1939 *September 5:* Suspension of all editorial and publishing activity due to outbreak of World War II.

September 16: Occupation of Niepokalanów by the German army.

September 19: Arrest of Father Maximilian and his confreres by the Wehrmacht and subsequent spoliation of Niepokalanów by the Nazis.

September 21: Imprisonment of the saint and confreres at Lamsdorf.

September 24: Transfer to Amtitz.

November 11: Transfer to Ostrzeszów.

> *December 8:* Father Maximilian, with permission of the German authorities, distributes holy Communion to his confreres; on this feast day of our Lady, the friars are released from prison.

1940 *December:* Publication of the only issue of *Rycerz Niepokalanej* during the war.

1941 *February 17:* Second and definitive arrest of the saint with four other fathers by the Gestapo. Imprisonment in Pawiak jail, Warsaw.

> *May 28:* Transfer to the Oświęcim concentration camp (Auschwitz).

> *Toward the end of July:* Saint Maximilian offers to take the place of Francis Gajowniczek, condemned to death by starvation.

> *August 14:* After at least two weeks in the starvation bunker, the saint is killed by a lethal injection of poison, possibly around 12:50 P.M., on the vigil of the Feast of the Assumption. His body is then cremated.

1971 *October 17:* Beatification as a confessor of the Church (white crown of virginity) by Pope Paul VI in Saint Peter's Basilica, Rome.

1982 *October 10:* Canonization as martyr of charity (red crown) by Pope John Paul in Saint Peter's Square, Rome.

The above is based on the following two works of Father Jerzy Domański: I dati storici della vita del P. Massimiliano M. Kolbe (*Historical data for the life of Father Maximilian M. Kolbe, Rome, 1973*) *and* I dati più importanti del "Diario delle Messe" del P. Kolbe (*The more important dates of Father Kolbe's* Mass Register, *Rome, 1974*), *first published as articles in* Miles Immaculatae, *volumes 9 and 10 respectively, and then apart as numbers 5 and 6 in the series* Quaderni della "Milizia dell'Immacolata", *sponsored by the International Center of the MI, Rome.*

Introduction

Saint Maximilian's devotion to the Immaculate and dedication to the ideal of the MI he lived so fully are proverbial. To the same degree, perhaps even more precisely in reference to its affective aspect, he cultivated devotion to the Eucharist. His express declarations of intent in this regard are few. Fortunately, there exist many, many testimonials to his great love, veneration, and respect for the Blessed Sacrament, a love already fervent during childhood.

These testimonials were recorded during the investigations preceding his beatification and canonization and published in summary form in the *Positio super virtutibus* (Rome, 1966) and in various collections (typescripts) preserved in the Archives of Niepokalanów, Poland, namely: "Documents concerning Fr. Maximilian M. Kolbe" (Declarations of Confreres and of Persons outside the Franciscan Order) (1953, 1958, and 1979); "Accounts of Fr. Maximilian Kolbe by Religious and Laypeople" (1969); and "Depositions of Fellow Prisoners" (1970).

All this vast material, with so many Kolbean eucharistic pearls (which ought not remain buried in archives), has been utilized here. It is perfectly evident, once this has been pondered, how in direct proportion to our saint's growth in devotion to the all holy Mother of God his devotion to the most Blessed Sacrament matured and became perfect, how in fact his priesthood came to resemble more and more that of the great High Priest. For it was the Immaculate who taught her knight how to honor and love Jesus in the Blessed Sacrament. To use his favorite phrase, she taught him to love Him with her heart.

In the first part of this study, my aim is to present Father Kolbe as a priest, and on this basis to describe, subsequently, how he celebrated Mass and adored the most Blessed Sacrament, and in the last section to recount his instructions for the Militia of the Immaculate in regard to the Eucharist.

I

SAINT MAXIMILIAN—PRIEST

Saint Maximilian Mary Kolbe worked in the vineyard of the Lord a relatively short time, just twenty-three years (1918–1941). But he lived his priesthood in a manner so profound and so Catholic, united so intimately with Christ the Priest and with his contemporaries, that he has become, to cite Cardinal Leo Duval, "the beacon for priests throughout the world" (*BMK*, p. 66).

Providentially, and not without forethought on his part, Pope Paul VI chose to beatify Father Kolbe in 1971 during the deliberations of the synod of bishops on the ministerial priesthood. "At a time", declared the then Cardinal Karol Wojtyła, "when so many priests were questioning their 'identity', Fr. Maximilian Kolbe stood up in our midst to answer, not in the format of theological dialogue, but in that of his life and his death. For him it was enough to be neither more nor less than his Master in giving witness to the 'greatest love' " (*P*, p. 20).

During the beatification ceremony, Pope Paul declared:

> Is not a priest "another Christ"? And was not Christ the Priest redemptive victim of the human race? What a glory, what an example for us priests to

behold in this new Blessed, a spokesman for our consecration and for our mission! What counsel in this uncertain hour when human nature will so often presume to assert its rights over against our supernatural call from Christ to give ourselves totally to Him in following Him! And what consolation for His beloved, noble, united, faithful ranks of good priests and religious . . . ! (*OR*, October 18–19, 1971).

Father Kolbe wrote no treatise, perhaps not even a single article, on the priesthood. All his recorded discourses were addressed to religious brothers. With priests, he spoke only in private and what was said is mostly unknown to us. But throughout his life, the priestly spirit, nurtured over the years in the shadow of the tabernacle and kept warm by the Immaculate Heart of Mary, shone brightly. It was she who inspired him, still only a subdeacon, to found the Militia of the Immaculate (MI). In the program of the MI, Father Kolbe found not only a stimulus, but the source of strength for living his priesthood to the full.

The Priestly Program of Saint Maximilian

Before sketching the priestly program of Saint Maximilian, it is worth recalling how he lived his ordination. The few notes he made at that time show how greatly he prized the grace of priesthood and how consistently he strove to be worthy of this.

Informed on April 9, 1918, by his rector, Father Stephan Ignudi, that he would shortly be ordained, he wrote in his diary: "O Immaculate, my Lady, help me to prepare myself well for so important an occasion. As I ponder this, I feel in some ways a certain consternation, but in others an ardent desire for a moment so long sought. I record all this, so that in the future, whenever I read these lines, my fervor will be enkindled ever more" (*SK* II, 988 B, p. 732). "Under the guidance of the Immaculate, the best of Mothers", he made the preparatory retreat, taking as his text a book by Archbishop Anthony Grasselli, O.F.M. Conv., *Esercizi Spirituali al clero secolare e regolare* (A retreat for secular and regular priests, Rome, 1894) (*SK* II, 988 B, p. 733).

After being ordained a priest, he wrote as follows on the first page of his *Mass Register*: "By the mercy of God through the Immaculate, the 28th of April, 1918, . . . in the Church of Sant'Andrea della Valle by his Eminence the Cardinal Vicar Basil Pompilj, I was ordained a priest of our Lord Jesus Christ" (*SK* III, 1336, p. 804). Father Kolbe always considered his priesthood a grace freely given and for which he held himself unworthy. "Who am I, O Lord God, that thou hast brought me thus far?" (2 Sam 7:18) was the inscription on the holy cards from his first Mass. On August 30 of the same year, he reminded himself: "God has called you to the priestly state and to religious life, because 'he has had a special love' for you, solely out of his own goodness, notwithstanding your own ingratitude" (*SK* II, 987 D, p. 697).

How much his heart burned with priestly zeal can be inferred from the intention of his first Mass, celebrated in the Church of Sant'Andrea delle Fratte at the altar of the Apparition of the Immaculate. He celebrated this neither for his parents nor his relatives nor for those who had helped him to the altar, as is normally the case with newly ordained, but "for the conversion of Sarah Petkowitsch, of schismatics, non-Catholics, Masons, etc." (*SK* III, 1336, p. 804), an intention quite in accord both with the priest's call to convert men to God and with the program of the MI.

After ordination, Father Maximilian had but one concern: "to correspond adequately with so great a grace and so exalted a dignity" (*SK* I, 19, p. 32), a concern reflecting his favorite law of action and reaction in equal measure. Similarly, the exhortation of Cardinal Pompilj, given in writing after the ordination rite: "*sit odor vitae tuae delectamentum Ecclesiae Christi* [May the fragrance of your life be the delight of Christ's Church]" (Archives Niepokalanów) was an added stimulus for this.

The entire sacerdotal program of Saint Maximilian was permeated by the virtue of faith, so characteristic of him and so evident in all his conduct: "Without doubt at the heart of all his activity," attests John Drucki Lubecki, "there was a deep, supernatural faith" (*Pos.*, p. 787). "I had the impression", another layman, the convert Francis Yamaki, relates, "that he was 'the Faith itself'" (*Pos.*, p. 737).

Father Maximilian firmly believed that the priest is "another Christ". During the retreat in preparation for the subdiaconate, he made this resolution: "Be Christ" (*SK* II, 966, p. 640). And he underlined these words three times. Thereafter, he spared no pains to become as perfectly like Him as possible. On April

21, 1918, Father Kolbe noted: "The concerns of the Sacred Heart of Jesus are your concerns" (*SK* II, 987 D, p. 696). Forgetting himself, he gave himself entirely to the cause of Christ. And because Christ had consummated His priesthood in the sacrifice of the Cross, he above all sought as priest to act "through the cross, through suffering, through sacrifice" (*SK* II, 982, p. 662). On May 20, 1918, three weeks after ordination, while meditating on the crucified Savior, he resolved: "The priest is another Christ. Preach Jesus Christ, and Him crucified, by word and example" (*SK* II, 987 C, p. 690), as did Saint Paul the apostle.

As Christ was concerned about His Father's business (cf. Lk 2:44) and sought above all His Father's glory, so Father Kolbe, from his first days as a priest, adopted this motto to express the main goal of his rule of life: "the greatest possible glory of God" (*SK* II, 971, p. 653). He often remarked: "Saint Ignatius did all for the greater glory of God [*ad maiorem Dei gloriam*]; and we must do all for the greatest glory of God [*ad maximam Dei gloriam*], because God deserves such" (Fr. Joseph Pal, *Pos.*, p. 824). In 1919, while praising the zeal of his brother, Friar Alphonse, for the glory of God, he lamented that "there exists in our day a very serious epidemic of indifferentism affecting not only laymen, but religious as well", although "God is worthy of infinite glory". Not being able to give him that great a glory—we are, in fact, creatures—he exhorted, "Let us at least strive to contribute, as much as we can, to making that glory as great as possible" (*SK* I, 25, p. 44).

For his part, Father Kolbe would do everything in his power to remain ever faithful to this youthful pledge. Countless subsequent declarations are more than eloquent testimony to his constancy of purpose: "In his every action he sought only the glory of God" (Fr. Anselm Kubit, *Pos.*, p. 596); "He lived only for the Savior" (Joan Kowalska, *Pos.*, p. 479); "He loved God above all else" (Br. Pelagius Poplawski, *Pos.*, p. 541). In this context is best understood the inscription on his other ordination holy card quoting a saying of Saint Francis: "My God and my all". On one occasion, meditating on this motto, he posed this thought-provoking question: "Jesus sacrificed Himself wholly for you, what about you?" (*SK* II, 987 D, p. 696). As Cardinal Wojtyła stated, Father Kolbe truly is "the priest who conceived his priesthood as a total consecration to God after the example of Christ" (*P*, p. 14).

"The glory of God", explained Saint Maximilian, "consists in the salvation of souls (practically identical). Salvation, then, and the most perfect sanctification of the greatest number of souls redeemed by Jesus at the costly price of His death on the Cross (beginning with ourselves) must be our lives' sublime ideal: all this to bring the greatest joy to the Sacred Heart of Jesus" (*SK* I, 25, p. 44). Such is the scope of the MI, as recorded in his *Rule of Life*: "The maximum glory of God through the salvation and most perfect sanctification of oneself and of others" (*SK* II, 971, p. 653). Pondering Christ's cry on Calvary: "I thirst" (Jn 19:28), Father Kolbe was moved to conquer all for Christ. On one occasion, he interpreted the cry of Christ thus: " 'I thirst' for souls; give them to me, O priests!" (*SK* II, 965, p. 933).

But from the beginning of his priesthood, he was convinced that the most important factor in the apostolate is the holiness of the apostle, since one can share with others only from one's own abundance; or somewhat better put, with holiness, one gives God free rein for his own generosity. Consequently, in his *Rule of Life*, he resolved initially: "I must be a saint, the greatest possible", and then later: "First, give yourself over entirely to your own sanctification, and so you will be able to give yourself entirely to the sanctification of others [*Totus primum sibi et sic totus omnibus*]" (*SK* II, 971, p. 654; *Pisma* V, p. 61), "from your superabundance", as he added at times when recalling this maxim (e.g., *SK* II, 980, p. 661). He repeatedly underscored the necessity of a profound interior life for the apostolate.

The other discovery of Father Kolbe during his youth, one which, when applied later in life, would constitute the secret of his success in sanctifying himself and in the apostolate, is union with the Immaculate, as such the Mediatrix of all graces. Informing his mother in 1918 about his priestly ordination, he confided:

> I acknowledge gratefully that this event was a gift obtained through the intercession of the Immaculate, our common Mother. How many times during my life, especially at its more important moments, have I experienced her special protection! Glory, then, to the Sacred Heart of Jesus, through Her who

was conceived without sin, who is the instrument in the hands of a merciful God for the distribution of graces. <u>In Her, therefore, I place all my confidence for the future</u> (*SK* I, 19, p. 31).

To give to the Immaculate a completely free rein in his sanctification and in his apostolate, he consecrated himself totally to her as her instrument, mindful that Jesus from the Cross "had given Her to us and us to Her" (*SK* III, 1145, p. 326). The greater part of his *Rule of Life* deals with this consecration.

> Remember always that you are the property and absolute possession of the Immaculate, unconditionally, limitlessly, irrevocably; whatever you are, whatever you have or can do, all that you do . . . belongs completely to her. . . . You are an instrument in Her hand; hence, do only what She wills; accept all from Her hand. Fly to Her in everything as a child to its own mother; entrust all to Her. . . . All the fruits of your activities depend on union with Her, in the same way as She is the instrument of the mercy of God. . . . I can do all in Him who strengthens me through the Immaculate (*SK* II, 971, pp. 653–54).

Father Kolbe made unrestricted consecration to our Lady the essential condition for achieving the scope of the MI. "There is no better way to approach Her Son than through Her" (*P*, p. 135), declared John Paul II in Seibo no Kishi. Effectively, the Pope here put his stamp of approval on the Marian way outlined for all by the Founder of the MI.

With Saint Maximilian's Marian piety is conjoined a great devotion to the Sacred Heart of Jesus. This is evident throughout the program of the MI, founded "to extend to the maximum the blessed Kingdom of the Sacred Heart of Jesus" (*SK* III, 1331, p. 785) and in which "the one stimulus is love without limit for the Sacred Heart of Jesus, in order to unite to Him through the Immaculate, in the most intimate manner possible, the greatest possible number of souls" (*SK* III, 1369, p. 835). As a priest, he recalled the promise made by Jesus to Saint Margaret Mary Alacoque, particularly venerated in the Roman Seraphic College where he studied: "Priests who cultivate a lively devotion to the Sacred Heart of Jesus will acquire the art of guiding souls to repentance, even the most obstinate" (*SK* II, 987 B, p. 682; cf. *SK* II, 962, p. 617). How often he himself repeated before the altar this ejaculation: "Gentle Heart of Jesus, I fervently beg you: make me love you, but make me love you always more" (*SK* II, 987 B, p. 687 and passim).

Saint Maximilian perceived the essence of total consecration to the Immaculate in obedience to her will, always identical, thanks to her Immaculate Conception, with the will of God. Hence, he resolved in his *Rule of Life*: "Your rule is obedience—the will of God through the Immaculate", and he added: "You are an instrument in Her hand; therefore, do only what She wishes; accept everything from Her hand" (*SK* II, 971, pp. 653ff.). Her will is disclosed in holy inspirations, especially at prayer, in the circumstances of life so arranged by God as to render the accomplishment of the work entrusted to each of us both possible and easy, but with maximum certainty via the will of those who possess authority in the Church. We fulfill the will of God through the Immaculate, in the light of her Immaculate Conception and of her *fiat* at Nazareth and at Calvary, as she would fulfill this in our place. Father Kolbe established the MI on the foundation of "holy obedience" (*SK* III, 1248, p. 579), especially to the Pope, the rock of the Church, as he always emphasized. He himself lived by obedience, marveling greatly at how the Immaculate would achieve her ends via one's superiors.

Although Father Kolbe applied these principles to all engaged in the apostolate, particularly to members of the MI, he maintained that they were above all relevant to priests, apostles par excellence. Thus, while striving to propagate this movement among all the faithful, he took special pains to spread it among priests and clerics and, in fact, initially recruited for the MI from their ranks. In the statute of the first center composed of Franciscan priests, Father Maximilian underscored the prime duty of every member "to seek to be an exemplary priest-religious, in particular as regards work in church" (*SK* III, 1370, p. 841). By means of the MI, Saint Maximilian hoped to reinvigorate the priesthood. In his cities of the Immaculate, he established minor seminaries to prepare future missionaries to conquer the world for Christ: "legions of religious priests, humble and poor, for the Immaculate and at Her side—ready for anything, for suffering, for humiliations, for missions, including the most difficult, unto total exhaustion, and unto death" (*SK* III, 1183, p. 396).

Bishop Ladislaus Miziolek synthesized Father Kolbe's apostolic program thus: "His spirit and his apostolic orientation are without doubt distinctively priestly; his religious vocation gave to this apostolate the depth of holiness and the broad vision of catholicity, transcending parochial and diocesan frontiers, embracing not only his own nation, but the whole world." Even more—it should be added—the Militia of the Immaculate, the flower of the Franciscan spirit, shaped this vision so deep and so broad. Although the statements of Saint Maximilian on the priesthood are few, "in his dedication to apostolic work, that is to say, to the spread of the kingdom of God in the world and in the implementation of this apostolate," to quote again Bishop Miziolek, "Father Maximilian provides, in our opinion, a splendid example for the ministerial priesthood, sharing in a special way the mission of Christ in the Church" (*HD,* p. 257).

The Priesthood of Father Kolbe in Practice

In describing the priestly ideals of Saint Maximilian, it is impossible not to mention his consistency in the application of principles. It is only logical, then, to consider next his priesthood in practice, in his daily life, so as to understand better the eloquent title the Church has given Father Kolbe: "Saint Maximilian, Priest", as well as the fruitfulness of his Marian-apostolic ideal.

In 1922, Reverend Roman Tartyllo met Father Maximilian for the first time at Grodno. As Father

Kolbe seemed very young, he asked him if he was yet ordained a priest. Father Kolbe, "mentioning the date of his ordination, replied that he was just a beginner, but that he desired to fulfill the will of God and to serve the Lord as zealously and as well as possible 'with the modest talents given him' ". On observing him over a number of years, Reverend Tartyllo came to admire deeply his zeal, his unswerving energy, his dedication to the cause of the Immaculate, and, in particular, his simplicity and humility—not making the slightest concession to personal comfort. "Truly," he concluded, "an exceptional priest, an exemplary religious, a holy man".

The catholicity, too, of Saint Maximilian, reminiscent of apostolic times and of the example of Saint Francis Xavier and his esteem for every soul, has caught the attention and won the admiration of all. "Since the time of St. Francis Xavier," added Reverend Tartyllo, "he is perhaps the first missionary who in obedience to his vocation and to the dictates of his great faith and ardent love has walked in the footsteps of that great Saint" (*Rel.*, p. 275). "He was", affirms Cardinal Julius Döpfner, "an apostle in the full sense of this term. He was quickened by an ardent missionary zeal that took him to Japan and India, and kindled in him a longing to conquer the whole world and all men for the Immaculate" (*BMK*, p. 395). Mindful of the revelation of Jesus to Saint Bridget "to be prepared to suffer much more than she had already endured for each single soul, if only to save it" (*SK* II, 966, p. 641), he was ready to make even the greatest sacrifice, even if only to conquer a single soul. After just one year of intense missionary labor with his confreres in Japan, he was successful in baptizing one citizen of that country. When this man declared: "If you had not come, I would still have been pagan", the founder of the MI remarked: "In this confession there is such sincerity and gratitude toward the Immaculate and toward us, her instruments, we spontaneously thought that even if none other than this man had been converted, all the effort so far expended, and even far greater sacrifices, would have been worthwhile, so long as they concerned a soul" (*SK* I, 483, p. 887).

Notwithstanding his wide-ranging plans, in practice, Father Kolbe focused his attention on specific situations toward which the will of God pointed. He concerned himself with existing persons, just as the well-known Mother Teresa of Calcutta does today in the practice of charity. "Do not overlook", he noted during the retreat of 1937, "any occasion to spread the kingdom of the Immaculate by example, by prayer, by suffering (humiliation), by the word, with the pen, and so forth" (*SK* II, 983, p. 664). On the other hand, he had not the faintest resemblance to an employee in religious garb, content merely to perform assigned tasks. For him, every situation was a field for apostolic endeavor, whether a train or a ship, a hospital or a prison. Persons whom he met he recognized as being sent by the Immaculate for him to serve in their need. "His sacerdotal zeal brought him to visit persons far from the Church and from the Faith, to draw them to the true Faith and to a Christian life", attests Bishop Joseph Gawlina (*Pos.*, pp. 78ff.), recalling his visits to masters of Masonic lodges, Protestant ministers, bonzes, etc. "I live for souls alone, this is my mission", he affirmed before his visit to the critically ill minister plenipotentiary of the Japanese government at Warsaw (*SK* II, 530, p. 24). In this declaration, he made perfectly clear his total availability as a priest.

Father Kolbe gave preference, it should be stressed, even during periods of heaviest involvement with the mass media, to activities strictly priestly, and this despite the problems his poor health frequently posed for such a preference, particularly for preaching. This is well illustrated during 1920 and 1921 at Zakopane sanatorium, where he was recuperating. Anna Wojtas, a nurse there, recounts:

> Each time that I so much as hinted at someone's spiritual need, he hastened to offer his priestly services to the sick, even if awakened at night—and this happened frequently—at times during snow or thunderstorms, often enough when he himself was running a fever. He would go without a coat, literally propelling himself to the place where some young life lay expiring. For example, during a thunderstorm, I informed him that there lay dying in the sanatorium a nonbeliever, named Krajewski, who did not want to hear the word confession so much as mentioned. . . . Well, what did Father Maximilian do? He rose very quietly from his bed so as not to disturb the other patients in the dormitory, went to the chapel to obtain the viaticum, and under a torrential downpour ran uphill along a muddy path toward the sanatorium "Bratniak". He returned suffused with joy because he had

succeeded in reconciling a dying woman with God (*Rel.*, p. 141).

While at Grodno, he sometimes rode farm wagons to distant villages to celebrate Mass and visit the sick. He heard confessions in church as did the other fathers (cf. *Dok.* II, 1, p. 254; *Rel.*, p. 55). In Niepokalanów, especially in the early years, he would confess 60 or more faithful in a single session (cf. *Alph.*, pp. 246, 256, 330). In Pawiak, he ordered a retreat in preparation for Easter (*Zez.*, p. 31). When recuperating in the concentration camp, he had a cot near the entrance door and there confessed prisoners, even at night, and many there were who took advantage of this service (*Zez.*, p. 68). Similarly, as a priest, he knew so well how to minister to those condemned to death in the starvation bunker that a locale such as that, commonly regarded as a place for blaspheming, was transformed into a chapel (*Zez.*, pp. 1ff.).

Father Kolbe "as a priest fulfilled his duties with the greatest zeal, seriousness, and holiness" (Rev. Vladimir Obidzinski, *Pos.,* p. 128). His wisdom and goodness, reflecting that of the Immaculate, attracted souls. This facilitated his success in the apostolate. "It was worth the effort", attests Alexandra Amerska, recalling her experiences at Grodno,

> to cross the river Niemen (where the Franciscan church was located) to hear the word of God from the mouth of this priest. There flowed from him a spiritual strength, that of love. One could sense his desire to help poor souls and carry them to God. He was an excellent confessor, because he understood

human misery and showed souls the way to the Mother of God, our mighty patroness and most loving Mother. A great number of penitents frequented his confessional, and at times it was necessary to wait considerably; but to wait patiently was worth it, because he filled the soul with a wealth of spiritual insight often sufficient for a lifetime. Father Maximilian loved children, so often unruly and mischievous; he understood them, and hence they flocked to him en masse. He smiled, chatted cordially and patted them on the head. He always encouraged them to love our Lady, because She is our Mother (*Rel.*, p. 1).

How much Father Kolbe prized this pastoral work is evident in a discourse of 1939, delivered on the occasion of the silver sacerdotal jubilee of a confrere at Niepokalanów:

A quarter-century of priesthood means consecrating and absolving for a quarter-century, that is to say, celebrating over nine thousand Masses and forgiving thousands of faithful. In addition, it means sowing the word of God, both in church and in private conversation with souls, preparing them for that last walk into eternity. All this exemplifies how much is involved in parochial work. . . . How great the results each of us knows. Simply tremendous! How many souls, thanks to priestly zeal, have approached God and been saved! How many souls in heaven will testify about those who helped them reach their final destination! Such persons will enjoy an immense gratitude, and a love so much the greater as their sacrifice was greater. A quarter-century is a period during which a priest accomplishes very much for the salvation of souls. Saint Augustine said: "If you save a soul, you will be assured of salvation." What should be said of him who has saved countless souls? (*CK*, September 4, 1939).

The founder of the MI did not restrict his efforts to the immediate apostolate. He recognized the effectiveness of modern inventions, such as the press, the radio, television, etc., for communications. Noticing how diligently the enemies of the Church utilized these on behalf of wicked and false causes, he became "the apostle of modern means of communication" (*P*, p. 58). He began during 1922 with an obscure monthly, *Rycerz Niepokalanej* (The Knight of the Immaculate). After 15 years, this work at Niepokalanów had expanded into one of the largest Catholic publishing houses, with seven periodicals, one mass circulation daily, all printed on the presses of the house. In 1938, he inaugurated the MI radio station and took the occasion to announce the forthcoming use of television in the cause of the Immaculate. The year 1930 saw the first issue of a periodical in Japan, which quickly reached a press run of 65,000 copies. All this Kolbean activity was, in the judgment of Cardinal Wojtyła, "truly and properly catechetical", "with a very modern approach" (*P*, p. 72). With these modern means, Father Kolbe "fired Poland with love for God and for the Immaculate" (*Pos.*, p. 476), an accomplishment duly acknowledged by the Polish episcopate. In Japan, his activity contributed to an increase of conversions.

Saint Maximilian organized and launched an itinerant apostolate, and in support of this also recruited friars to work in the mass media, "so as to touch the hearts of men more effectively by way of the living word" (*SK* I, 382, p. 654) and to conquer them by the testimony of their lives. "These friars trained to use the pen, the microphone, the screen and other skills, are to travel outside the enclosure of Niepokalanów and approach souls personally via retreats, missions, conferences and confessions, organize and visit the MI 2 [second degree]" (*SK* I, 382, p. 654). Father Kolbe not only sent the fathers to preach home missions and retreats, but in the eastern part of Poland, endangered by sectarianism, he also organized visits by religious brothers, in pairs, to the villages to distribute MI publications. He did the same in Japan with *Seibo no Kishi* along the roadside.

In view of this, John Paul II has numbered Father Kolbe among the "architects of pastoral care" (*P*, p. 94), along with Saints Vincent de Paul, John Vianney, and John Bosco, all of whom met the needs of their time. Similarly, he has numbered him among the greatest home missionaries, such as Saints Ignatius Loyola, Alphonsus M. de'Liguori, and Louis Grignion de Montfort, "brilliant, practical men . . . whose example we must constantly recall if we would enlighten and save our brothers" (*P*, p. 131).

Invaluable, too, was the advice Saint Maximilian customarily gave to priests. One pastor, Reverend John Lipski, recounted during the process of beatification:

> Through correspondence, I received from Father Kolbe suggestions and motives for promoting the spiritual welfare of the faithful, and I must say that

his advice was very useful and efficacious for that end (*Pos.*, p. 270).

In the letters he wrote me, he included the saying *per Mariam ad Jesum* [to Jesus through Mary] and observed that because Mary all holy is Mother both for Catholics and for Orthodox, it was easy for the latter to reenter the Church. ... Inspired by his writings, I dedicated myself with great confidence to seek the conversion of schismatics in my parish and had the consolation of receiving into the Catholic Church about three hundred Orthodox schismatics (*Pos.* 1957, pp. 137ff.).

Reverend Marian Jacewicz declared himself particularly grateful to Father Kolbe for the counsel and encouragement given him at the start of his priestly ministry among the Orthodox in eastern Poland. Asked by him to suggest the saying for a holy card, Father Kolbe gave him this text from Isaiah: "Behold, here I am; send me" (Is 6:8) and added: "And the Lord has sent me to labor, that there might be one flock and one shepherd." He also suggested that "I read attentively an editorial in *Rycerz Niepokalanej* entitled 'The Pope and the Blessed Sacrament', and that I put these counsels into practice, in view of the reconciliation of eastern Christians with the Catholic Church, because this method would without doubt produce salutary fruit." Later, Reverend Jacewicz realized that this was the method suggested by Bishop E. Bougaud in his work *The Church*.[1] After the war,

---

[1] Vol. 4 of the five-volume work *Le christianisme et les temps présents* (Orléans, 1872–1874); with four later editions and also translated into German and Italian (1923).

during a visit to Niepokalanów, he stated that the method when applied had positive results in his pastoral work (*Rel.*, pp. 39ff.).

Saint Maximilian sought to recruit for the modern apostolate not only priests but religious brothers and Catholic laity as well. He succeeded in attracting to Niepokalanów hundreds of young men for the religious brotherhood. (In 1939, these numbered over 600, counting candidates.) He formed them in the spirit of the MI and employed them brilliantly in a vast and multifaceted missionary activity, as printers, pilots, technicians. At times, he exhorted his priestly confreres not to neglect their priestly duties and not to busy themselves in activities the brothers could perform.

Realizing the fruitfulness of the MI ideal, Father Kolbe promoted it with special care among priests and seminarians and encouraged them to spread it among the faithful. Before the war, there were enrolled in the ranks of the MI almost a million faithful from every stratum of society and all walks of life, forming in fact an "army set in array" (cf. *LP*, p. 24), although more often than not the founder stressed the nonorganizational character of the movement. The contribution of the MI laity to the Church in Poland was enormous. How many letters were received at Grodno and afterward at Niepokalanów from priests, once they were convinced that the MI facilitated their pastoral work. Reverend W. Lewicki of Kamionna wrote in 1926 that in his parish there were more than 1,000 members of the MI, and "thanks to this, conduct has improved, faith has been deepened, devotion increased, as also the reading of good literature" (*RN* 1927, p. 18). Another pastor stated in 1936: "I now see clearly how much good the Immaculate accomplishes through the Militia and the miraculous medal, because church attendance has increased, faith and conduct have improved and the people have become better" (*RN* 1936, p. 358). Of that period and context Professor E. Weron, SAC, could write: "The entire MI movement was focused on the responsibility of the laity and aimed at employing them, not only in defense of the Church, but in rendering their presence . . . in the world vital." In a word, it aimed at "the maturity of the laity" (*HD*, p. 306).

Reverend Tartyllo, observing the apostolic activity of Saint Maximilian at Grodno, admired how well he could use his time. He wrote:

> Truthfully, it is difficult to grasp how anyone in the space of 24 hours could plan and execute so many tasks, without neglecting anything. Holy Mass, the breviary, meditation, retreats, composing articles for *Rycerz Niepokalanej*, the printing of the review under very difficult circumstances, the accounts, correspondence, etc. Almost every day it was necessary to stop the sun in its course, crying out like Joshua: "Sun, do not move!" From this is evident the presence of God's help through the intercession of the Immaculate Mother (*Rel.*, p. 128).

In all his many activities Father Kolbe was effectively sustained, not only by his talent for organization, but also by the faithful observance of a resolution made in youth: "*Serva ordinem et ordo servabit te* [Keep order and order will keep you]" (*SK* II, 971, p. 653).

A Life of Prayer and Sacrifice

Notwithstanding his "activism", Saint Maximilian did not succumb to frenetic activity. He always stressed—in theory and in practice—the primacy of the interior life. He reminded himself and all engaged in it that the apostolate

> is a collaboration (if such is the correct word) with God himself in the work of perfection, of sanctification. . . . In view of this work, therefore, the Savior himself expressly commanded his apostles: "Remain in me and I in you" (Jn 15:4–6). . . . The fruitfulness of work, then, does not depend on ability, on energy, on money, although these, too, are gifts of God useful in the Catholic apostolate, but solely and exclusively depends on the degree of one's union with God. Should this decrease, or if such be weakened, the other means will avail nothing (*SK* III, 1071, p. 156).

> Eloquent sermons and work divorced from prayer bear no fruit (*SK* II, 965, p. 635).

Father Kolbe took pains to keep himself united to God through the Immaculate. He persevered in the state of grace. He often remarked: "I do not fear death, but I do fear sin" (*Pos.*, p. 456). And so he made every effort to make the love of God increase in himself and to pray ever more perfectly. In his apostolate, he always gave pride of place to God; hence his works grew and bore fruit, despite the fact that on so many occasions he was forced to use faulty tools. The person and work of Father Maximilian, concludes Bishop Miziolek,

> warn against the currently fashionable oversociologization of priestly life, with a consequent elimination of its most essential components: the supernatural call, holiness and participation in the mission of Christ. The person and work of Father Maximilian are an appeal for priests to attend to their authentic sanctification and to consecrate themselves fully to the cause of Christ and of the Church (*HD*, p. 263).

It is worth dwelling at length on the prayer life of Saint Maximilian. Before receiving the diaconate, he had realized that prayer "is an obligation of primary importance for the clergy", particularly prayer that is "humble, confident, persevering", and that it "is more efficacious than words or good example; from prayer flow conversions" (*SK* II, 968, p. 646). He resolved: "I must pray insistently and perseveringly; with a fervor ever greater. And through me God will work miracles.... The knees, not the intellect or the pen, give efficacy to action.... Prayer before and after every activity" (*SK* II, 965, p. 635). Father Kolbe, notwithstanding his multiple occupations, dedicated much time to prayer, engaging all the energies of his soul in it, whether in an hour of adoration or in the short prayers before meals. Celebration of Mass was the high point in his life of prayer. During the day, he would often interrupt his work to visit the chapel, there to adore Jesus in the most

Blessed Sacrament with all the ardor of which he was capable. He did not forget ejaculations and good intentions. Brother Luke Kuzba affirms: "Each day for Saint Maximilian seemed to constitute a prayer of the best kind, whose irresistible outlet was before the most Blessed Sacrament" (*Dok.* II, 1, pp. 143ff.). His confrere, Bishop Joseph Palatucci, O.F.M. Conv., observed in him "throughout his life a spirit eminently eucharistic" (*Pos.*, p. 62).

And, it should be added, Saint Maximilian acquired this spirit in the school of the Immaculate. He looked to her example and strove to act as she would have in his place. He made frequent contact with her by means of good intentions, above all before any new engagement, by means of ejaculations, or at least a glance at the statue always standing on his desk (and during his sea voyages in his cabin aboard ship), through frequent recitation of the Rosary and that dialogue of love, often wordless, wherein he strove to learn her will and implore the graces to fulfill it well. In his personal notes is often found the exhortation: "Let yourself be led by the Immaculate. . . . With joy. Be Hers evermore" (*SK* II, 981, p. 661).

Cardinal Paul Bertoli, former prefect of the Congregation for the Causes of the Saints, reflecting on the tremendous fruitfulness of Father Kolbe's priestly labor and on his eucharistic and Marian devotion, declared: "Because he was a man of faith and prayer, he found in the Eucharist and in devotion to Mary Immaculate, whom he loved and whose hero he was, the source of his apostolate." And in his Niepokalanów, he saw not only a great apostolic center, but above all "the cradle of prayer and piety" (*M*, p. 112).

Thanks to his intimate union with God, Saint Maximilian preserved, even at the peak of his magnificent pastoral activity, a profound humility, which kept him from being condescending to other priests, even the youngest. It is God who acts and gives his graces through each priest. In 1939, a newly ordained priest, Reverend Marian Jacewicz, came to Niepokalanów. With the intention of attending himself, Father Maximilian immediately invited him to celebrate Mass for all the friars. Before beginning, Reverend Jacewicz, conscious of the sanctity of Father Kolbe, asked him to bless him and to bless the priestly apostolate awaiting him. He recalls:

> I thought while kneeling that he would extend his hands over me and bless me, and then give me his hand to kiss. Instead, evidently wishing to place in relief my priestly dignity, even if quite recent, he immediately knelt before me, blessed himself with the sign of the cross and said "*Nos cum prole pia benedicat Virgo Maria* [May the Virgin Mother mild bless us with her holy Child]." I rose surprised and much moved, but above all edified by his humility (*Rel.*, p. 40).

His spirit of sacrifice had its origin in his relation to the Eucharist and was the implementation of his youthful resolutions to follow Jesus crucified. Together with prayer, he considered sacrifice the most effective means of apostolate. With patience, without complaint, indeed with surprising calm, he bore the physical sufferings associated with his lung disease and with the torments of prisons and concentration camps during the war, as likewise the spiritual trials and suffering frequent, above all, during his apostolate in Japan. Willingly he undertook priestly toil, in any form whatsoever. He practiced Franciscan poverty in its extreme form and absolute obedience to superiors. Quite correctly, Father Stephen Krajewski writes: "In encounters with Saint Maximilian, the continuous sacrifice of his own life was experienced by others to their great enrichment, and won to Father Maximilian countless hearts" (*HD*, p. 267).

The spirit of sacrifice led Father Kolbe to the very heights of heroism, to the giving of his own life for a condemned man at Oświęcim. Saint Maximilian, priest, became after the example of Christ, the High Priest, a victim. This he had asked of Christ in prayer during his first year of priesthood when in the Church of Saint Anastasia Martyr in Rome he celebrated Mass according to this intention: "*pro amore usque ad victimam* [for a love to the very point of being a victim]". Cardinal Wojtyła has put the point nicely:

> Father Kolbe celebrated Holy Mass, and hence it is a "truism", that is, it is quite true to say, that he lived the sacraments. But we would like to refer rather to the period of his life in which he no longer celebrated Holy Mass, namely, during his first imprisonment and then during the second and final incarceration in the concentration camp of Oświęcim. He offered, in fact, to enter the starvation bunker in place of a brother Pole, his companion in prison. But

it is precisely in this period when he no longer celebrated Holy Mass in the sacramental sense, that he celebrated to the very last, with his life and with his death, the holy sacrifice. In that way, Father Kolbe participated in that great sacrament of our faith which is the Eucharist; and this became in him the fulfillment of his vocation and of his life (*P*, p. 73).

This, too, is significant. During his life, Saint Maximilian did not consciously stress his priestly character. That he was a person consecrated to God one could easily infer from the habit he always wore. And the life of sacrifice, which he himself lived and which he required of those consecrated to the Immaculate, he inspired with love. To a confrere unhappy over too many sacrifices and who said that God did not need heroism from us, he replied: "God does not need anything from us, because he is happy in himself, but the soul which loves him is ready for anything" (*Dok*. II, 1, pp. 243ff.). But when, in the concentration camp, he was no longer allowed to wear the habit, and at times when asked who he was and why he sacrificed without regard for his own person, he replied: "I am a Catholic priest." Thus he spoke to Doctor Rudolph Diem, a Protestant, who marveled in wonderment and admiration that Father Maximilian did not wish to accept his offer to transfer him to the hospital, rather suggesting another in his place (*Pos.*, p. 578). So, too, he replied to the camp commandant, Karl Fritzsch, after asking to be the substitute for a man condemned to death by starvation (*Pos.*, p. 572). His priestly character impelled Father Kolbe to conform himself ever more to Jesus

Christ, until he too became a priest-victim. "This final sacrifice of Father Maximilian", attests Cardinal Julius Döpfner, "had a character totally sacerdotal" (*BMK*, p. 39).

This is Saint Maximilian Mary, priest—a priest according to the heart of Jesus, formed by the Immaculate, with the traditional marks of a priest, yet at the same time appealing to his contemporaries. "He was an ideal priest", Reverend Vladimir Obidzinski, pastor of the parish of Pawłowice, of which Niepokalanów was a part, testified of him (*Pos.*, p. 401). "In the concentration camp," recounts Ladislaus Lewkowicz, "he was acclaimed after his heroic death a hero-martyr, a man of God, a true priest of Jesus Christ" (*Pos.*, p. 368). In the words of Cardinal Wojtyła, during the 1971 synod of bishops, Father Kolbe turns "our minds to that truly evangelic image of the priesthood" (*Pos.*, p. 11). "Maximilian Kolbe, precisely as priest," so Cardinal Döpfner told priests, "sets before us both the measure and the model of priesthood. . . . In fact, he lived that pastoral love which the Second Vatican Council proclaims to be the essence of priestly life" (*BMK*, p. 41).

As the beatification of Father Maximilian was greeted by Cardinal Duval, so now even more his canonization may be acclaimed "as the dawn in the renewal of priestly life" (*L*, p. 259). And indeed, the canonization of Father Kolbe confirms the hope expressed some time ago by an Italian bishop, Monsignor Andrew Casarano: "The wonderful example of Father Kolbe will succeed in overcoming the apathy of the times, will strengthen the faith of Catholic peoples, will renew love for the Virgin most holy, make clear to the embittered all the beauty of the Catholic priesthood, bring back the erring to the maternal womb of Holy Church" (*LP*, p. 8). In this sense and in this context, he himself continues to work in heaven "with both his hands", faithful to the promise he made on earth.

II

THE MASS IN THE LIFE OF THE SAINT

In the writings of Saint Maximilian Mary, there is to be discovered but a single description of a Mass celebrated by him, namely, that on the day of his sacerdotal ordination, concelebrated with the ordaining bishop, Cardinal Basil Pompilj, and his fellow ordinands. These are the pertinent passages from his diary and his letter to his mother (informing her of his ordination).

> The morning of the 28th [of April, 1918]. . . . Toward 7 A.M. we left the College for the Church of Sant'Andrea della Valle. There after vesting, together with the others, I prepared for my first Holy Mass (*SK* II, 988 B, p. 733). [After the sacramental rite of ordination the newly ordained priests celebrate Holy Mass.]

> It was a moving event: notwithstanding differences [of nationality], we were as one united by the bond of Catholic faith and in the fraternal love of Jesus. . . . After the ordination, we were priests and, in addition to the other prayers of Holy Mass, with his Eminence the Cardinal we pronounced the words of consecration (*SK* I, 19, pp. 30ff.).

> After the consecration tears came to my eyes, but I had to control my emotions and recite the prayers of the canon (*SK* II, 988 B, p. 733).

This eucharistic sacrifice began a series of Masses that, except when manifestly impossible, the saint celebrated every day, at first in churches and chapels of Rome and elsewhere in Italy, then in his homeland and in the missions. That initial freshness, the same faith and devotion, even emotion attendant on his first Masses, was ever sensibly present when he celebrated. No trace of routine, so common a failing of repeated acts, was ever noticed in him. To paraphrase the Psalm he recited each time he ascended the altar (Ps 42:4), God in truth prolonged and gave joy to his spiritual youth.

It is instructive to study in detail how the founder of the MI celebrated Mass, so as to be able to understand still better his priesthood and his entire spiritual life and to appreciate in the light of his example that inestimable treasure the priest bestows on mankind. Perhaps it is no mere coincidence that some of the holy cards distributed after his first Mass bore this eucharistic theme: the chalice with host, held by an angel, and inscribed thus: "Behold the goodness of our divine Savior and His love for men." Father Kolbe desired to enrich all men with this treasure.

Two sources are available to us for learning how Saint Maximilian celebrated Holy Mass: his *Mass Register* and the testimonies, quite numerous, of those who attended his Masses.

The Mass Register

It was once the custom among priests, particularly those who had completed their studies in Rome, to keep a record (or register) of all Masses celebrated from the day of their ordination. This custom reminded them of their main duty as priests and of the very great blessing they bring the human family in celebrating holy Mass. Finally, it guarded them against possible forgetfulness and neglect.

Saint Maximilian kept his *Mass Register* faithfully from the day of his ordination until the end of his life. Each page of this register listed the Masses for a single month with the following notations: number of the Mass within the entire series, the day of the month and feast falling on that day, the intention, and the place, church, and date of celebration. In addition, at the top of each page in the center is noted the current month and year, at the left, the year of priesthood, and at the right, the year of birth. At the end of the first year are the words: "*Deo per Immaculatam gratias* [Thanks to God through the Immaculate]." Occasionally, for lack of time, one or another notation was omitted, but Father Kolbe never forgot the sequential number. After the last date, February 14, 1941, is the number 7,695 and at the top of the page: 23rd year of priesthood and 48th of birth. (The final total should be higher. He celebrated Mass on the next three days, i.e., until February 17, 1941, when he was taken to Pawiak prison.)

Up to the present, very little attention has been paid this register consisting of two small volumes in octavo, with at times almost illegible notations, with abbreviations, and written mostly in Latin. It was assumed that nothing of interest or of use for attaining a better understanding of the saint could be found there. In fact, an in-depth analysis and a comparison with his *Diary* and other writings are most informative. First, Father Kolbe's *Mass Register* makes possible the precise resolution of all chronological questions concerning his priestly life. Next, it contributes to a deeper understanding of his interior life. "Where your treasure is, there also will your heart be" (Mt 6:21), said the Lord. From the intentions of his "free" Masses, from the votive Masses chosen, from the altars more often selected for celebrating Mass, one can learn what was Father Maximilian's treasure and what goal he consistently pursued.

THE FIRST MASSES

On the first page of his *Mass Register*, there is a kind of dedication, the creed of a newly ordained priest (cf. p. 6 of the original). Above the dedication, Father Kolbe drew a simple cross in red ink, to underscore, as it were, that the priest draws strength from the Cross of Christ, that with the Cross he is united to the sacrifice of the Mass, and that it is the Cross that shows the way to sacrifice.

Particularly significant are the places and intentions for the first four Masses (after the ordination Mass) of Father Kolbe. For his first Mass, he chose the Church of Sant'Andrea delle Fratte. "The next day", he wrote in his *Diary*, "I celebrated Holy Mass at the altar where the Immaculate deigned to appear to A. Ratisbonne and what is more (a complete surprise) the votive Mass of the Miraculous Medal. Assisting was Father Peter Joseph Pal (a Romanian) and serving was Father Jerome Biasi (from Trent, Italy), both spiritual friends of the Immaculate" (*SK* II, 988 B, p. 734). And his intention in celebrating? Not, in the first place, for his family and friends, as is the custom of newly ordained, but as we have seen "for the conversion of Sarah Petkowitsch, of schismatics, of non-Catholics, of Masons, etc." (*SK* III, 1336, p. 804). The significance of the choice of church, of votive Mass, and of intention becomes clear in view of the fact that when still only a subdeacon (October 16, 1917), Father Maximilian founded a pious association under the title Militia of the Immaculate (MI), with the scope of "working for the conversion of sinners, of heretics, of schismatics, etc., and above all of Masons, and for the sanctification of all, under the protection and through the mediation of the Immaculate" (*SK* III, 1330, p. 781). He designated the miraculous medal as its distinctive emblem and as one of the means highly recommended for this end. He had been inspired to undertake this work on January 20, 1917, the 75th anniversary of the day on which the Immaculate appeared to Alphonse Ratisbonne, as can be seen on the miraculous medal. Father Pal and Father Biasi were the first members of the MI, the closest to the heart of the saint. One mystery remains: the identity of Sarah Petkowitsch, whose name also figures in a separate list entitled: "Memento for the Living", and where, in addition, it is underlined. The conversion of this person seems to have held special importance for him. He was convinced that God would more likely hear him on so solemn an occasion. Perhaps he remembered the example of his favorite saint, Saint Thérèse of the Child Jesus, who on the day of her first Communion prayed for a poor person she had met during a walk with her father.

The intention of Father Maximilian's next Mass seems even more extraordinary. He celebrated this in the Basilica of Saint Peter, April 30, 1918, at the altar of the tomb of the Prince of the Apostles—as a votive Mass in honor of Saints Peter and Paul—with the petition: "For the grace of the apostolate and of martyrdom for me and for my confreres in the College [*pro gratia apostolatus et mart. pro me et confratribus in Collegio*]" (his confreres were the friars resident at the International Seraphic College of the Friars Minor Conventual, Via S. Teodoro, Rome, where the saint lived while studying philosophy and theology, *SK* III, 1336, p. 804). The thought of martyrdom never left our saint. One day, he asked Father Pal for a memento (remembrance) in his Mass that the good Jesus would grant him the glory of martyrdom (*Pos.*, p. 823). He reminded him of this request in 1920 (*SK* I, 46, p. 93). On May 20, 1918, Father Kolbe celebrated Mass in the Catacombs of Saint Callistus, at the altar of Saint Cecilia. The significance of this he himself recognized as important, noting the fact in red ink. One of his Christmas Masses that year he offered "*pro amore usque ad victimam* [for love to the point of becoming a victim]", that is, asking for the love that makes one a divine victim. With one of the first members of the MI, Father Pal (perhaps with others as well), he made a pact to pray for each other "to obtain the grace of martyrdom" (*SK* I, 46, p. 93), which he recalled afterward at least three times. Reading the writings of the saint especially dear to Father Maximilian, Thérèse of Lisieux, so absorbed in heroic desires, and the biography of Saint Gemma Galgani, whose motto he often quoted: "Love without limit", certainly had a great influence on his decisions. But the original source of this intention is to be discovered more probably in his childhood vision of two crowns, one white, the other red, which he confided to his mother and which she revealed after his death as a martyr at Oświęcim.

On May 1, 1918, Father Kolbe celebrated Holy Mass at the Franciscan Basilica of the Twelve Apostles (where each year he participated with enthusiasm in the novena to the Immaculate) at the tomb of the holy apostles Philip and James, whose feast occurred that day. He did not record his intention, but the next day he visited the place of death of the apostle of the Gentiles, at the Basilica of Saint Paul Outside the Walls, where he celebrated Mass at his tomb—again a votive Mass of Saints Peter and Paul—"*pro Papa* [for the Pope]". Saint Maximilian always showed the greatest respect and esteem for the Vicar of Christ. One of the witnesses during the informative process on Father Kolbe declared that "in his attachment to the Holy See he showed himself a true disciple of Father Ignudi", a very saintly man, counselor and confessor of several popes, and Father Kolbe's rector, "on that point [of attachment to the Holy See] worthy of admiration" (*Pos.*, p. 62). Father Ignudi always spoke with feeling of his audiences with Pius X and Benedict XV. The attacks of the Masons on the papacy, particularly violent during 1917, provided the stimulus for the founding of the MI. During his meditation of January 15, 1918, Father Maximilian resolved: "Defend Jesus, His Church and the Pope, by every means available to you" (*SK* II, 987 B, p. 680). And he did indeed defend these treasures to the very end of his life.

THE INTENTIONS

His next Masses Saint Maximilian celebrated according to the intentions assigned by his superiors; once or twice a month, sometimes more often, he would have a "free" Mass, that is, one he could celebrate for an intention chosen by himself. And it was precisely in these "free" Masses that he disclosed the recesses of his heart.

On March 1, 1919, a Saturday, he chose the votive Mass of the Immaculate Conception "to thank the most Holy Trinity, the Sacred Heart of Jesus and the Holy Spirit for all the graces accorded the Immaculate, above all the grace of the Immaculate Conception." This unusual intention is often noted in the *Mass Register* of the founder of the MI, particularly during the early years of his priesthood. In addition, every day, at the "Memento of the Living", he thanked "the most Holy Trinity, the Heart of Jesus and the Holy Spirit for all the graces granted to the Immaculate . . . and above all for the grace of the Immaculate Conception, with all those preceding, accompanying and following it" (*SK* III, 1336, p. 805). Father Alphonse Kolbe, brother of Maximilian, confirms this, adding that he "promoted the practice" (Alph., p. 267).

Father Maximilian's favorite dogma was that of the Immaculate Conception of Mary, in which he saw, in the light of her self-definition at Lourdes "I am the Immaculate Conception", not only exemption from original sin, but the fullness of grace and the entire divine plan for her introduction into the economy of salvation, into the work of conversion and sanctification of souls. On this truth he grounded his Militia of the Immaculate so as to incorporate, he said, the dogma into life. Cardinal Karol Wojtyła, during the Mass celebrated for the diamond jubilee of the founding of the MI at the place of its foundation (the Seraphic College, Rome), expressed this beautifully. "It is here that Father Kolbe discovered the mystery of the Immaculate, and he discovered this not only as the greatest beauty of the created universe, but above all as a force, a most powerful energy which he wished to share with others as well. To that end he directed all his labors and gave it the name of Militia of the Immaculate" (*P*, p. 74). Noticing that the Mass had the particular character of thanksgiving (*eucharist*, etymologically, means giving thanks), he thanked God in it for various graces, but in a special way for the grace of the Immaculate Conception at the starting point of our salvation, which grace in its effects is ever present in our sanctification.

With this intention is linked, in the Kolbean diary, another which in later years gradually supplanted the first and which Father Maximilian formulated thus: "according to the intention most pleasing to the Immaculate" or "according to the intention of the Immaculate", or, still more succinctly, "personal for the Immaculate". Father Alphonse comments: "He prayed according to the intentions most pleasing to her, so that as soon as possible she might become in practice Queen of all souls, singly and collectively" (Alph., p. 267). At the beginning of the "Memento of the Living", Father Maximilian prayed: "I. For each and every person whom the Immaculate in particular chooses; . . . II. According to all the intentions of the Immaculate and for each one singly" (SK III, 1336, p. 805). Father Maximilian believed that one could implore graces most easily from God through the Mass in union with the Immaculate, by sharing her sentiments and intentions, because her will is the faithful reflection of the will of God.

At the "Memento of the Living", he also prayed every day "for the grace to increase devotion to the Immaculate without measure, whether intensively or extensively" (SK III, 1336, p. 805), believing that in such a way men would more easily draw closer to Jesus. The Militia of the Immaculate has a special responsibility to spread this devotion. Its act of consecration to our Lady concludes with the following petition:

... that I be a fit instrument in your immaculate and merciful hands for introducing and increasing your glory to the maximum in all the many strayed and indifferent souls, and thus help extend as far as possible the blessed kingdom of the Most Sacred Heart of Jesus. For wherever you enter, you obtain the grace of conversion and growth in holiness, since it is through your hands that all graces come to us from the Most Sacred Heart of Jesus (*SK* III, 1369, pp. 835ff.).

For this Father Kolbe added in the memento this intention: "for the Militia of the Immaculate 'intensively', as regards its internal structure, blessings and indulgences, and 'extensively' for each and all who are or will be its members" (*SK* III, 1336, p. 805).

He applied his "free Masses" according to the intention of the Immaculate on the more important feasts, especially Marian, and before more important events and undertakings, for example: at the beginning of the year; before the provincial chapter; before departing for Japan; before founding Mugenzai no Sono; before pronouncing his fourth vow declaring himself ready for any assignment; before his journey to India; on his return from the German concentration camp in 1939, etc. Whether a given event went as he desired or not, he was willing and happy to accept the consequences, convinced that this was best, because it was the will of the Immaculate, and equally persuaded that the Mass had obtained the desired result, perhaps in the form of strength to bear adversity.

What especially catches the eye in Father Kolbe's

Mass Register is the almost total absence of any Masses celebrated for his personal intentions or for those of his family. At most, one or two might possibly be considered such. For the Feast of the Annunciation of the Blessed Virgin Mary, feast day of his mother, he noted: "For the intentions of the Immaculate", or sometimes only: "*personal*", but to be interpreted—as he himself expressly wrote, March 25, 1930—"personal for the Immaculate". He had given all to the Immaculate, even his own intentions (cf. *SK* II, 971, p. 654); hence, in this he was consistent. This does not mean he did not love his relatives or friends, but that he held to a principle adopted during the retreat of 1920: "Interest yourself solely in Her, in Her veneration and Her affairs, and leave yourself and your dear ones in Her care" (*SK* II, 971, p. 654). The all holy Mother knows how to recompense those who have honored her, and for the rest, her will for each is always the best. For her feast day, he wished his mother "one thing only: to fulfill as perfectly as possible, always and in everything, the will of God, through the mediation of the Immaculate, beyond which there is nothing more sublime, nothing more perfect" (*SK* I, 496, pp. 911–12; cf. *SK* I, 12, p. 19; *SK* II, 569, p. 79).

On a separate list entitled "Memento of the Living", together with the explicitly Marian intentions already mentioned, there are two other general ones: "V. For all, and for each of those to whom I or my family, or who to me or my family, have done, said or thought anything, good or evil, or will do, say, think anything in the future. VI. For all those presently alive, or who will live in the future, and for each of these singly"; and thereafter 83 more or less detailed intentions added during the course of his life. At the beginning, his parents and brothers are named, then no. 5: all his "relatives, friends and enemies and each of these singly"; no. 6: "all those commending themselves to our prayer, and each of these singly"; no. 7: "all those for whom I should and can [pray] and each of these singly"; no. 8: "all non-Catholics and each of these singly (for their conversion)"; no. 9: "all Catholics and each of these singly (for their sanctification)"; then for childhood friends, seminary companions, his rectors, professors, and superiors; no. 48: "for him who paid my fare to Lwów; no. 49: "Poland, Romania, Austria, Russia, Germany, Ukraine, Czechoslovakia, Danzig"; no. 50: "France, Italy, San Marino, Lithuania"; then he mentions a certain Jew; no. 58: "scholars and students"; no. 59: "those entrusted to my care, spiritual or otherwise"; no. 77: "O.F.M."; no. 78: "brothers who were, or now are, or will be employed in the publishing house"; no. 79: "Mission of the *Crociata Francescana*" [Franciscan Missionary Crusade]; no. 80: "*Rycerz*, MI, publishing house" (*SK* III, 1336, pp. 805–8). Everywhere his great priestly heart is transparent in a love embracing those near and far, friends and enemies present and future, able to acknowledge and repay even the smallest service; a love that would have wished, with the Mass, to draw down the most abundant blessings of God on all. Recounting, on one occasion, to the friars how he always remembered all of them, those who were, are, or would be in Niepokalanów, he remarked: "It is a pleasant duty for me" (*CK,* April 3, 1938).

There are on this list, moreover, the names of two deceased persons, Thérèse of the Child Jesus and Gemma Galgani, with the notation: "For their glorification" [*Pro glorificatione*]. Subsequently, Father Kolbe would write of Saint Thérèse in an article entitled "The Patroness of the Missions": "Even before her beatification and canonization, after having read a short biography of her, I said: 'I promise to make a memento [remembrance in prayer] in every Mass for your beatification and canonization, and on your part you will take care of my mission'" (*SK* III, 1263, p. 635). How each partner profited from this agreement is now well known. And how delighted Father Maximilian was to be able, by chance, to participate in the beatification of Gemma Galgani, May 14, 1933 (*SK* II, 991 S, p. 902).

At the request of the dying Father Emil Norsa, O.F.M. Conv., a convert from Judaism (and composer-musician), he joined to his own intentions at Mass those of Father Emil: "1. For the Holy Father; 2. for peace in the world; 3. for the conversion of the Jews" (*SK* III, 1113, p. 256).

Above all, Father Kolbe remembered at Mass the dying and the dead. After enrolling in the "Pious Union of the Dying", on July 17, 1919, he celebrated a Mass "for the dying" and, underlining this intention, he notes at the foot of the page: "After my death, contact 'The Pious Union of the Dying' [Church of the *Transitus*, i.e., Passing or Dying, Porta Trionfale, Rome], so that they can appoint another in my place to celebrate Masses for this intention." Every year on July 15, he celebrated Mass for the dying.

In the "Memento of the Dead", as recorded in a separate list, he prayed as follows: "1. For all those whom the Immaculate wishes to be remembered, and for each singly"; "2. For all those, and for each singly, to whom I or my family, or who to me or my family, have done, said or thought anything, good or evil." He then recommended, by name, specific persons or groups (54 in all), among whom were relatives; confreres in religion and their relatives; members of the MI; his physician at Zakopane, Doctor Burdygan; and, at the end—after his brother, Father Alphonse—Archbishop Aloysius Bondini, O.F.M. Conv., his beloved spiritual director, who had written him, September 30, 1935: "Should you learn of my death, do not forget to remember my poor soul in your Holy Masses and in your other prayers" (*SK* II, 985, pp. 674–75). Only in the next life will we learn how many persons obtained the grace of conversion and of sanctification or hastened their passage to glory through the holy Masses of Father Maximilian.

MASSES ON THE MARIAN FEASTS

The founder of the MI, as his *Mass Register* makes clear, solemnly celebrated the Marian feasts, above all the Immaculate Conception, Presentation of the Lord (known formerly as the Purification of Our Lady), the Apparitions at Lourdes, the Annunciation, the Assumption, the Nativity of Mary, Our Lady of the Rosary, Christmas, and the solemnity of the Sacred Heart of Jesus. Generally, on these feast days, he celebrated Mass for his own intentions. On Saturdays, as "the day of the Mother", he used the votive Mass of the Immaculate Conception, in accord with a privilege granted his order (indeed, it pained him very much if his confreres neglected this). On other days, when the rubrics allowed, this was the votive Mass he celebrated by preference. The reason is already evident. Intriguing is the fact that, just before his imprisonment at Pawiak (February 17, 1941), Father Maximilian thrice celebrated the votive Mass of the Sacred Heart of Jesus. It is not known whether he recommended himself to the Savior's mercy, or if he offered himself as victim, but probably he had both intentions in mind, sensing his imminent imprisonment.

The devotion of Father Maximilian to the Queen of Poland is also exceptional. From 1925 on, the date of the solemn confirmation of this feast, we find that he offered a free Mass on the third of May. On his return to Poland from Rome, he journeyed to Jasna Góra (Częstochowa), and there, August 18, 1919, he celebrated at the altar of the Crucified and, the next day, before the miraculous image "in thanksgiving through the Immaculate Conception". So too, when he was planning the establishment of Niepokalanów, just before the provincial chapter that was to decide the matter, he went to Częstochowa and celebrated before the miraculous image "according to the intention most pleasing to the Immaculate, and that She might deign to convert the whole world as soon as possible" (*SK* I, 174, p. 304). On May 3, Father Kolbe was accustomed to tell his confreres that, with the help of the Poles, the Immaculate wished to conquer the whole world for herself and through that conquest for her Son. For the occasion, he planned activities designed to promote that goal.

Father Kolbe celebrated Mass where he could, or wherever he had been assigned, but, when free to choose the place, he preferred to celebrate in a Marian sanctuary or at an altar of the Blessed Virgin Mary or of one of the Marian saints. We know from his *Register* that he celebrated in the Valley of Pompeii, before the image of Our Lady of the Rosary, June 4, 1918; at Trinità dei Monti (Holy Trinity Church, Rome) before the image of the Mother Most Admirable, July 15, 1918; in the Franciscan Basilica, Kraków, at the altar of the Sorrowful Mother, and more frequently at the altar of the Immaculate, where, in 1922, he found the money necessary to pay the cost of printing the first issue of the *Rycerz Niepokalanej*; at Gidle, August 17, 1919; in the Marian sanctuaries of his order at Poznań, April 4, 1926; and at Kalwaria Pacławska (February 14, 1928; June 4, 1933; August 15, 1937); at Lwów, April 8, 1929, where, as a student in the minor seminary, he had vowed to fight for the Immaculate; at Lourdes, January 30, 1930; at the tombs of Saints Stanislaus Kostka, Rome (November 14, 1918), Anthony of Padua (January 24, 1930), and Francis of Assisi (January 27, 1930; September 7, 1933). On these occasions he ordinarily celebrated a free Mass. He was deeply disappointed that because of an accident he could not celebrate

Mass, January 31, 1930, in the chapel of the miraculous medal in Paris, but only in the residence of the Vincentian Fathers.

From the *Register*, it is evident how Father Kolbe made every effort to celebrate Mass. He was often sick, but only once did he note, between January 18 and February 3, 1922 (during a particularly difficult period): "I did not celebrate Mass because of illness." In Japan, for some time, he had such painful abscesses that he could stand on but one foot at a time. Nevertheless, he celebrated even in those conditions, assisted by two friars. At times, when traveling, he could not celebrate; thus from June 26 to July 3, 1930, he noted: "*Sine Missa in curru ferreo per Siberiam* [without Mass on board a train across Siberia]"; so also from August 14 to 24, 1930, on his return to Japan by the same route. At the end of the trip, he had an unpleasant surprise. At Pusan, counting on a four-hour layover between the arrival of the train and the departure of the boat, he had planned to say Mass, but no one could direct him to a Catholic church. A policeman informed him that in all of Korea there were but three such churches. And so he exclaimed spontaneously: "When will the Immaculate take possession of this magnificent country and introduce into it the Kingdom of her Son?" (*SK* I, 280, p. 423). Today, interestingly, among the other churches at Pusan there is a Franciscan church, built by Koreans educated in the seminary of Mugenzai no Sono, founded by Father Maximilian. Indeed, there exists in Korea a custody [province in formation—TRANS.] of his order, dedicated to him, with six friaries and many churches.

Sometimes, during his sea voyages, he would rise very early to find a place at the altar. On June 1, 1932, while sailing for India, he began Mass at 3:30 A.M. On another occasion, there being no altar, he remained fasting until midday in the hope that the ship would dock in port before 1 P.M. (in those days the hour beyond which it was not permitted to celebrate Mass). On June 20, 1930, approaching Darien, he wrote in his *Diary*: "I still have a possibility [a little before 1 P.M.] of celebrating Mass according to the intentions of the Immaculate" (*SK* II, 991 B, p. 837). A day earlier, he noted: "Corpus Christi, but I did not celebrate Mass, as I was aboard ship" (*SK* II, 991 B, p. 836). In such instances, he would remark: "It is not to my liking, but the will of the Immaculate be done" (*SK* II, 991 G, p. 862).

HOW FATHER KOLBE CELEBRATED MASS

The *Mass Register* can hardly disclose the state of Father Kolbe's soul when celebrating holy Mass. Nor has our saint left any description thereof, except for one reference to the concelebration on the day of his ordination. In his writings he seldom speaks of the Mass. But in his *Notes* made during his retreats and daily meditations, particularly those dating from his early years, are to be found reflections and resolutions that, without doubt, guided him for the rest of his life.

First of all, there is evident the great respect given by Saint Maximilian to the Eucharist and the importance he attributed to it in life. In 1918, just over a month before his sacerdotal ordination, he noted: "The love of Jesus in the Blessed Sacrament above every other thing. He is our All" (*SK* II, 987 B, p. 686). And in later years he would remind himself during retreats: "The Eucharist is the strength of the soul" (*SK* II, 982, p. 663).

Next, Father Kolbe felt a great responsibility for keeping himself holy, so as to be able to celebrate holy Mass worthily. "Holiness", he wrote in 1918, "is necessary to celebrate Holy Mass" (*SK* II, 987 C, p. 691).

Another duty is preparing oneself well to celebrate and thanking Jesus after celebrating, as is fitting. Each day he would offer half the day as a preparation for Mass and Communion, and the second half as thanksgiving, mindful that "preparation and thanks consist in the fulfillment of one's duties" (*SK* II, 962, p. 611; cf. *SK* II, 987 I, p. 722). Nor did he forget the immediate preparation before and thanksgiving after Mass. Among other practices, he encouraged himself "to tell Jesus after Holy Communion what makes you suffer, to ask counsel, and to make thanksgiving" (*SK* II, 962, p. 618).

He cultivated good intentions and interior dispositions. "One of the better intentions", he wrote, "is the ardent desire to acquire strength and renew one's strength so as to fulfill more easily the will of God" (*SK* II, 963, p. 623).

Saint Maximilian wished that the Mother all holy might accompany him to the altar. "The Immaculate", he wrote on June 8, 1918, the Saturday after the solemnity of the Most Sacred Heart of Jesus, "knows the secret of most intimate union with the Heart of Jesus" (*SK* II, 987 C, p. 691). "Receive Jesus", he resolved Christmas Eve 1918, "and accept everything from His hands, with the same dispositions which the all holy Virgin Mary had at the moment of the Annunciation: 'Behold the handmaid of the Lord; be it done to me according to your word' " (*SK* II, 987 E, p. 703). He faithfully carried out her inspirations. In his *Mass Register*, there is a loose page in his handwriting, on which is written: "Our Lady manifests her will in all; listen and act in peace."

Significant is his resolution, Marian in flavor, made during meditation the last day of 1918, his first year of priesthood: "May Jesus live in you. Love for Jesus via fraternal love, that Jesus might live and reign in all. MI" (*SK* II, 987 E, p. 703). He knew that loving Jesus, with the strength of His grace and after the example of the Immaculate, would effectively illumine his surroundings, indeed, influence the entire world and conquer it for the Heart of Jesus, thus achieving as easily as possible the ideal of the Militia of the Immaculate. Throughout his life, Saint Maximilian, qua knight of the Immaculate, as the witnesses attest, united most intimately with Jesus, lived by His grace in a state of victimhood symbolized by the red cross on the first page of the *Mass Register,* spent himself for Jesus in his brothers, and fulfilled His will as faithfully as possible by keeping before his eyes the example of the Immaculate.

He also discerned the will of Jesus in the cry of the prisoner of Oświęcim condemned to death by starvation and at once offered to be his substitute. And when the commandant, utterly abashed, asked who he was, he replied, as it were, in a last echo of the first words of his *Register*: "I am a Catholic priest."

The Testimonials

Besides the *Mass Register*, there is still another source for learning how Saint Maximilian Mary celebrated Holy Mass, namely, the declarations of those who attended his celebration of the Eucharist, given privately or during the investigations preceding his beatification. These are quite numerous, because the comportment of the saint at the altar made a deep impression on everyone.

PRIESTLY DEVOTION

A typical first impression is given by Sister Felicity Sulatycka, of the Congregation of the Immaculate Conception. Her experience dates from December 1926, at Zakopane. She recounts:

> In my first meeting with Father Maximilian, I was struck above all by his faith. I had entered the chapel of the "Pelczarki" Sisters [Little Servants of the Sacred Heart] at Zakopane, where he was recuperating. Holy Mass had begun, and I was quite distracted. But very shortly, I was impressed by the manner in which this unknown priest celebrated Holy Mass and how this impelled me to pray. He was much absorbed in the sacred character of what he did, and this highly impressed me. I thought he

must be a holy priest. After Mass, I remained while he made his thanksgiving—which was recollected and long. On leaving, I asked the sister portress who he was and learned he was Father Maximilian, founder of the Militia of the Immaculate (*Pos.*, pp. 122ff.; cf. *Rel.*, p. 120).

In the celebration of Mass, Father Kolbe "showed much devotion, but also was quite normal: nothing bizarre", as his seminary friend, Father Andrew Eccher, noted (*Pos.*, p. 251). "A special devotion, but so natural", according to the testimony of a fellow missionary in Japan, Brother Cassian Tetich. So too, a layman, Eugene Srzednicki, states that "his comportment [during Mass] was natural, neither artificial nor theatrical" (*Pos.*, p. 320). He was punctual and as superior required punctuality in his priests (cf. Br. Damian Kluenjko, *Dok.* I, 1, p. 106). "He prepared himself", testifies Brother Lawrence Podwapinski, "with great care for Mass and celebrated Mass observing the rubrics and liturgical norms exactly, with the greatest recollection and profound absorption in the mystery of the most holy sacrifice. His thanksgiving after Mass lasted not less than twenty minutes and he was totally immersed in this prayer" (*Pos.*, p. 430). He took about thirty minutes to celebrate Mass with "his eyes downcast and his head a bit inclined" (Br. Samuel Piasecki, *Dok.* II, 2, p. 413), "tranquilly, neither rushing nor prolonging it" (Br. Ruffino Majdan, *Pos.*, p. 657). "He distributed Holy Communion quickly, but calmly, with great respect and devotion" (Br. Marius Leszczynski, *Dok.* I, 1, p. 144). Reverend Ferdinand Machay describes the

Mass Father Kolbe celebrated February 1, 1930, in the Polish Church in Paris: "I served this Mass, and to the present day I consider this service to have been a retreat without a sermon: so much did his recollection and devotion edify me" (*Rel.*, p. 69).

He kept the eucharistic fast strictly. At times, while traveling, he would not eat till midday, if he had any hope of still celebrating Mass. A very eloquent testimony is that of the physician A. Wasowicz: "When I was called one night to attend Father Kolbe in an emergency and prescribed a medicine in water to ease his pain, the patient asked for the time, and, learning that it was a few minutes past midnight, he chose to suffer, rather than not be able to celebrate Mass" (*Pos.*, p. 464).

Many pondered the state of soul of the saint while celebrating Mass. Brother Benedict Mieczkowski stated in 1969:

> A long time has passed since I saw him celebrate the sacrifice of the Mass, but I always remember how, with the Sorrowful Mother, he lived the mysteries of the passion and death, and of the glorious resurrection and ascension of the Lord Jesus. This true priest was not only an official vicar of the Savior at the altar, he not only celebrated Holy Mass, as is commonly said, but he united himself intimately with Christ in this mystery of our redemption, offering as well to Christ the total gift of himself through the Immaculate, so renewing his unconditional consecration to her. In this mysterious union with the Mediatrix of all graces, and through her with Christ and with all the Church, is hidden the secret of his true greatness (*Dok.* II, 2, p. 260).

Other testimonies are more generic, but no less eloquent. "He celebrated Holy Mass with such devotion that one felt he was not a man, but Christ himself celebrating" (Br. Marius Leszczynski, *Dok.* II, 1, p. 144). "The fervor of a deeply spiritual man pervaded his entire person" (Fr. Florian Koziura, *Pos.*, p. 86). "His thought was entirely fixed on God" (Rev. Vladimir Obidzinski, *Pos.*, p. 408).

Without doubt, the heart of the saint during holy Mass burned with love in response to the love of Jesus in the Eucharist, an ardor reflected in the color of his face. One June evening, during the eucharistic devotions in honor of the Sacred Heart of Jesus in the chapel at Niepokalanów, a well-known Polish hymn was sung: "Your Heart, O Jesus, burns with love . . . and our hearts are cold as ice, in vain your passion's toil." On leaving the chapel, Father Maximilian remarked immediately to the friars: "It is not true that our hearts are cold as ice. Our hearts are alive and burning; they intensely love the Heart of Jesus. Hence, his toil was hardly wasted" (Brs. Luke Kuzba and Mansuetus Marczewski, *Dok.* II, 1, pp. 143, 167). Surely Father Kolbe loved Jesus, and, with the ardor of his love, set other hearts on fire, especially when celebrating Mass.

At times, Father Kolbe joined great personal sacrifices to the eucharistic sacrifice he celebrated, particularly during sickness, so that he became indeed a priest-victim. Once he confided: "Yesterday my blood pressure made my forehead ache so, and today I had to hold my head during Mass" (*CK,* February 14, 1933). On May 29, 1932, the day of his departure for India, Brother Romuald Mrozinski, a missionary, wrote from Nagasaki to Niepokalanów:

> Our dear Father Director suffers not only with heart and lung problems. Two months ago he also suffered from abscesses forming on his body, one after the other, sometimes two or three at once, causing tremendous pain. We well remember how, being unable to walk, he celebrated Mass assisted by two of us. We held him under both arms, so he could stand on one foot, the left, with the right foot suspended. But when the first leg went numb, it was necessary to lean on the other, in excruciating pain. Sometimes he would cry out in agony. One day, when we were bringing Father from his cell to the chapel, the ulcerated part of his body accidentally bumped the door and he fell to the floor in agony. For a few minutes, even with our help, he could not rise. We begged him not to celebrate Mass and to give himself and us only Communion, but he replied: "Somehow, slowly, I will celebrate, the Immaculate will help." . . . What an impression to see how the saints suffer; we will never forget this (*Dok.* II, 1, p. 191; cf. *SK* I, 391, p. 682).

EUCHARISTIC SHEPHERD

The testimonials relative to the eucharistic apostolate of Father Kolbe stemming from various periods of his priestly life are interesting. If during Mass he was so deeply recollected that no one and nothing besides Jesus seemed to exist for him, in fact, he did not forget the faithful who surrounded him; he embraced them with a loving glance, as though with that of Jesus, and ministered to their spiritual welfare.

When Father Maximilian was at Grodno, recalls the teacher S. Roszkowska, "young people from neighboring parishes flocked *en masse* for services held by him in the Franciscan church. When questioned why they did so, they answered that they wished to be present at the Holy Mass of the Servant of God and hear his sermons" (*Pos.*, p. 15). Sometimes, on Sunday, Father Kolbe went to villages far from Grodno, e.g., Kopciówka, to celebrate Mass especially for the elderly and for children. Immediately after his arrival by gig, he began hearing confessions and continued to the very last penitent, so that as many as possible might receive Communion with a pure heart. Then he would ascend the altar.

> After the Gospel, he preached from the altar. He spoke in a low voice, without rhetoric or gesticulation. I would not say he spoke eloquently, because he was more than eloquent, although not ornate. Notwithstanding the heat (in summer), no one slept, no one stirred. After Mass, Father Maximilian would treat of various matters with individuals, rushing no one in order to have his breakfast (T. Kostrzewska-Przanowski, *Rel.*, p. 55; cf. G. Gasiorowska, *Rel.*, pp. 34ff.).

So too at Niepokalanów and Mugenzai no Sono and in their environs, the saint made every effort, when he celebrated Mass for the people, to do so in a manner most apt from a pastoral point of view. "I often watched the Servant of God during Holy

Mass," recounts a neighbor of Niepokalanów, Jeanne Kowalska, "and I must say that no other priest I ever saw celebrated as he did. . . . He spoke to the people of the goodness of God, of his mercy; he desired to attract all to the Lord. In fact, he did draw all to prayer and to the service of God. He administered the sacraments with great devotion" (*Pos.*, pp. 472, 476). After Mass, he would handle various business affairs with the faithful, but rarely visited their homes, and then only for pastoral concerns. When, in 1928, Hedwig Jaczynska, wife of the administrator of Teresin, paid him a first visit and expected one in return, Father Maximilian replied: "Yes, we will meet, not at table, but at the Table of the Lord" (*Rel.*, p. 45).

It is worth noting that Father Maximilian "loved solemnity during the celebration of feasts, especially that of solemn Masses", as Reverend Bernard Hatada, of Japan, testifies (*Pos.*, p. 182). "He encouraged the use of liturgical chant", relates Father Florian Koziura, an enthusiastic promoter of Gregorian chant (*Pos.*, p. 86). But during solemn Masses he retained that recollection and devotion so characteristic of him during liturgical services.

More often, Father Kolbe celebrated Mass for his brothers in the cities of the Immaculate, to the great profit of their souls, particularly in what concerned the ideal of the MI. This he did with greater solemnity on Sundays and on feast days. This is how Brother Arnold Wedrowski recalls him:

> The Sunday sermons of Father Maximilian made an unforgettable impression on me, as postulant and then as novice. I remember them as [if from] yester-

day. After the meditation with the friars, he rose and, slowly, recollectedly, moved toward the altar. He genuflected with devotion and then behind the altar, in the sacristy, he prepared for Mass. His every movement was marked by a striking earnestness. When he came forth vested, his recollection kept the participants rapt in attention. The pronunciation of the words, the gestures, the expression of the eyes, all revealed this man to be living at the altar the very presence of God. After reading the Gospel, he kissed the holy Book, glanced for a moment at the religious, his beloved sons in the Immaculate, who left their kneelers to draw near the altar, so as to hear him better and see his gentle, piercing eyes, from which poured kindness, goodness and, above all, love. His first words generally were: "The Immaculate", or "Dear sons". He encouraged each of us to belong to the Immaculate, to love her as a son loves his mother, but infinitely more, and to exert ourselves to conquer for Her all other souls in the world. . . . The homilies of Father Maximilian were not long, about 10 minutes. . . . The last word, as far as I remember, was again: "The Immaculate", usually in the phrase: "Dear sons, let us be led by the Immaculate." After the homily he embraced all with his glance, at once kind and piercing. . . . (*Dok.* II, 1, p. 329).

The example of Father Maximilian and his talks on Mary united all to Jesus in the Blessed Sacrament. To Him he normally devoted a part of his homilies.

Toward the end of his days at Niepokalanów, Father Kolbe celebrated more often in the chapel of the sick friars. There, even more, he showed his fatherly kindness toward the brothers and revealed his union with Christ on Golgotha and on the altar. "His figure and his entire comportment stimulated devotion and recollection. All his gestures and actions exerted a strong influence" (Br. Innocent Wojcik, *Dok.* II, 1, p. 344). In the homily, he touched on the value of sacrifice. Jesus Christ, he said, without doubt, chose for the work of redemption the means most important and rich in merit, namely, suffering. Salvation, life, perfection, sanctity are on the Cross. Apart from the Cross, there is no salvation for the soul nor hope of everlasting life. With the suffering of love, we unite ourselves at the best possible moment with God and collaborate with Jesus for the salvation of the world. The infirmary of Niepokalanów bears the pure and best fruit, because, in suffering, one's own "ego" is melted as in the furnace and because "it is easier to be a martyr than to roast for years over the slow fires of suffering." Blessed the soul that grasps the value of suffering (cf. Br. Julius Grzybowski, *Dok.* II, 1, pp. 83ff.).

Knowing how the Eucharist strengthens the sick and kindles in them a love ready for sacrifice, Father Kolbe brought holy Communion to the cells of those who could not be present for Mass in chapel. When Father Mieczislaus Mirochna, a cleric whom he took with him on the Japanese mission in 1930, was recovering for two months in a Nagasaki hospital, he brought him holy Communion every day (cf. *SK* I, 303, p. 465).

The saint, both for his own devotion and for the welfare of other travelers, celebrated Mass during his journeys, for example, when in 1919 he was returning to his homeland from Rome in a Red Cross train, or on board ship, notwithstanding difficulties. At Easter of 1933, on board the SS. *Conte Rosso*, en route to Poland, he celebrated Mass publicly "at 11 A.M., with a brief homily on the end of man and on devotion to our Lady, the Immaculate". He told "the sailors that it is easier to save oneself, and entails far less suffering than to condemn oneself" (*SK* II, 991, p. 890). Sister Anna Zawadzka, a Franciscan Missionary of Mary, recalls how, in 1936, she returned with Father Maximilian from the Far East to Europe on the SS. *Victoria*. The saint asked her to be sacristan. He desired to celebrate at 4:30 A.M., before cleaning and other activities commenced, so as to be, given his nerves as he said, more recollected. In the end, he consented to 5 A.M. She wrote:

> Each day at this hour, he celebrated Mass. I readied everything for his Mass, and, together with my sisters, received from his hands Holy Communion. I drew great profit from this. I marveled at the devotion, concentration and affection with which Father Maximilian celebrated Mass, and, in my heart, quite spontaneously, I formed this conviction: "Truly, this is a holy priest." Notwithstanding Father's self-description as nervous, he was instead calm, quiet, affable, even at periods of searing heat or burning wind (*Rel.*, pp. 149ff.).

It is not necessary to relate—it is so obvious—that Father Kolbe, as Father Samuel Rosenbaiger narrates, "faithfully kept the holy days of obligation and saw to it that his subjects kept them too" (*Pos.*, p. 7).

One example suffices. Brother Mansuetus Marczewski relates:

> On one of the Sundays of 1929, a new candidate arrived in Niepokalanów. Father Maximilian asked him how long he had been traveling and whether he was well. After learning that he had not yet attended Mass, he ordered another postulant to accompany him to the parish church of Kaski [about 5 kilometers—3 miles—distant] to hear Mass, since the Masses in Niepokalanów had already been celebrated. When the candidate had gone, Father Maximilian told me that he could have dispensed him, but did not, so as to emphasize the importance of hearing Mass on Sunday (*Dok.* II, 1, p. 167).

During the war, when, at times, the Germans organized hunts for men after Sunday Masses, Father Kolbe on those occasions ordered the cloister opened to protect the faithful from deportation to Germany (Br. Cherubim Pawlowicz, *Dok.* II, 2, p. 355ff.).

CARE FOR THE HOUSE OF GOD

Recalling the stall at Bethlehem, Saint Maximilian, a lover of poverty, was not hesitant about celebrating Mass even in the poorest chapels. Brother Henry Borodziej recounts:

> How often we attended Masses celebrated by him at Niepokalanów in a poor chapel, and in Japan in an even humbler one. Simple tables nailed together served as an altar, and a platform of rough planks as a floor. No ornamentation, except a statue of the

Immaculate above the altar and still higher an image of the Sacred Heart of Jesus. This was symbolic of the ideal and faith of Father Maximilian that we must tend to Jesus through the Immaculate. To achieve this as much as possible, we must consecrate ourselves totally to the Immaculate, without limit or restriction, as her possession and property (*Dok.* II, 2, p. 605).

However, Father Kolbe cared for the cleanliness of chapels and churches, including poor ones. "Although the little chapel [in Niepokalanów] was very poor, it was maintained in the greatest cleanliness; the Servant of God deeply desired it to be clean and decorous" (Joan Kowalska, *Pos.*, p. 475). In Niepokalanów, "he required much of the sacristan; he called his attention to the dignity of his work, since he was permitted to handle the sacred furnishings of the altar" (Fr. Florian Koziura, *Pos.*, p. 306). Indeed, "the sacristy is concerned with Citizen Number One of Niepokalanów, the Lord, our elder Brother and Spouse of souls, present in the Eucharist, that He find himself at home among us and do much in our midst" (*SK* III, 1239, p. 553). Similarly, he commanded the sacristan in Mugenzai no Sono "to keep the chapel clean and to see that the sacred articles were handled in a manner befitting them" (Br. Romuald Mrozinski, *Pos.*, p. 696).

The saint was not opposed to splendid churches. "He often said", attests Father Florian Koziura, "that God and the Immaculate must be honored by the faithful in beautiful churches" (*Pos.*, p. 306). He once wrote: "Can their splendor ever be excessive, or at the very least worthy of such a Lord?" (*SK* III, 1059, p. 135). When projects for a church at Niepokalanów began to be discussed, he sent plans from Japan, constituting, as it were, a "credo" for the project. "Surely," he wrote, "the 'basilica' should be sufficiently ample and functional, but also austere and lovely in its proportions, all converging on a single aim: to save and sanctify the greatest number of souls possible through the Immaculate. In any case, only what is indispensable for that goal should be included." At Niepokalanów, I have seen the design of the church made by Father Kolbe himself: in the form of a hemicycle where all converges on the altar.

In the above-mentioned letter from Japan, the saint expresses his negative judgment on many churches that, despite their artistic merit, do not serve the ends of a house of God.

> How the tourists gape, passing from one church to another to admire masterpieces of art instead of adoring Jesus in the Blessed Sacrament! How these "things of beauty" at times distract from rather than invite to recollection and to prayer! How they frustrate the very purpose of the church itself! Similarly, how distracting the "musical concerts", to hear which so many persons flock to certain Roman basilicas! (*SK* II, 585, p. 99).

Father Kolbe, as Brother Henry Borodziej rightly observes, in the case of his Niepokalanów, "was in no hurry to build splendid churches, because, as he said, 'we must rather save souls, as quickly as possible, so that they consecrate themselves without reserve to

Her, and when they already belong to Her, out of love for Her they will erect the most magnificent sanctuaries'" (*Dok.* II, 2, p. 61) and honor in them her divine Son. This was also his view in regard to the sacred vessels and vestments. Once, in Niepokalanów, one of the friars fell ill, and the friary had nothing, not even a penny, with which to cure him. So Saint Maximilian, on reflection, called Brother George Dudek, at the time infirmarian and sacristan, and asked him how many chalices they had. On receiving the answer "two", he said: "Take a chalice from the sacristy, sell it in Warsaw and buy whatever is necessary for the sick friar." And when he hesitated, somewhat in amazement, the superior added: "To save a living temple, in which every day Jesus receives a friendly welcome, one can sell a sacred vessel" (Br. George Dudek, ibid., p. 63).

How the witnesses were affected by Saint Maximilian while he was celebrating Mass is apparent in the address of a religious brother of Niepokalanów, Brother Felicissimus Sztyk, to Father Kolbe after his death:

> I was so happy when I could serve your Mass. I sought out the occasion. I had the good fortune to serve you at your last Mass in Niepokalanów. On a postcard you wrote: "My dear son, I will put you once and for all in the Memento of the Mass along with the other intentions; all right?" (*SK* II, 715, p. 308). I was delirious with joy. Can there be any fortune better than to be remembered daily before God, in the prayer of greatest value, namely, the Mass, celebrated by one's most beloved Father?

Hence, when the "Memento for the Living" of your Mass approached, I projected myself mentally into your heart to unite with your fatherly prayer. I know you are faithful to your promises; hence, I have not the slightest doubt that today you pray for me before the throne of our Queen, so that I might pass happily through this vale of tears and be able to glorify with you the mercy of God and the maternal kindness of our Queen (*Dok.* II, 2, pp. 466f.).

Only a few material souvenirs of Saint Maximilian have survived. His body, burned in a crematory, is not included among these. But in the archives of Niepokalanów there remains his *Mass Register*, and, in his "old chapel", as also in the museum of Seibo no Kishi in Nagasaki, there are on display the chalices, chasubles, and stoles he used. Pilgrims visit there. During his visit to Nagasaki in 1981, Pope John Paul II paused in the museum of Seibo no Kishi to meditate on Saint Maximilian Mary the priest and to be inspired by him in celebrating, or assisting at Mass, with a faith and a devotion worthy of so great a mystery.

III

LOVE IN ADORATION

The exceptional devotion of Saint Maximilian to the Eucharist appears not only during his reverent celebration of Mass, but also in his practice of adoring Jesus in the Blessed Sacrament, a practice inherited from his parents and exercised to the very end of his life, a practice he promoted, whatever his circumstances. He is to be numbered, without doubt, among the most zealous adorers of the Most Blessed Sacrament the history of the Church has known. Love drew him to the altar. He realized that one could worthily honor the Sacrament of Love only with love. In the light of so many testimonies, let us consider this love of the saint that accompanied him throughout every stage of his life, from childhood to 1941, the year of his last contacts with Jesus in this sacrament and the year of his meeting with Jesus face to face after a martyr's death, to contemplate him and to adore him, with love, forever and ever.

During Childhood

In Pabianicé, "on Sundays and holy days (and in those times the holy days were more numerous) the Kolbes", Antonina Koch relates, "attended church, like everyone else, as a family, dressed in their best clothes and with a book of devotions in hand" (*Dok*. I). Usually they went to the Church of Saint Matthew in the old city, their parish church until 1907, or to the Church of our Lady of the Rosary in the new city, toward whose erection they contributed. Raymond, going to church with his parents, imagined himself at times accompanied by Saint Joseph and our Lady (cf. the letter of Marianna Kolbe to Niepokalanów, October 12, 1941).

Julius and Marianna Kolbe, greatly esteeming the value of the Mass, were, from the beginning of their marriage, in the habit of visiting the church in Zduńska Wola on weekdays as well at 8 A.M., summer and winter (Anna Kubiak, *Dok*. I); in Pabianicé at 5 A.M. during the summer (Anastasia Socha, *Dok*. I). In other seasons, the boys, before leaving for school, brought breakfast to their father and took his place at work as a weaver under the watchful eye of his partner, Lenicki, while he made a visit in church (Joseph Lenicki, *Dok*. I). Julius "received the sacraments frequently" (Martha Przedmojska, *Dok*. I).

The elder Kolbes "in Pabianicé belonged to the Third Order of Saint Francis, whose members held adoration of the most Blessed Sacrament in the parish church every Sunday throughout the day. Groups of men and women would adore Jesus in the Blessed Sacrament, taking turns for an hour each. Julius Kolbe organized and directed the adoration of the men" (Martha Przedmojska, *Dok*. I). He also "initiated and directed the adoration at the 'tomb of the

Lord' (the sepulcher)" during the sacred Triduum (Joseph Lenicki, *Dok.* I).

So too, the three sons of Julius and Marianna liked to attend church on weekdays. Recalling the years 1906 to 1908, Theodore Novak states:

> I did not know them personally, but always saw them in the Church of St. Matthew at the 5 A.M. Mass and at evening devotions.... I was much edified by their devotion and exemplary conduct. They prayed devoutly and sang well. Their complete recollection caught my attention, all the more so because by nature they tended to be vivacious. ... One day, leaving Mass, I genuflected on one knee only. Raymond approached me and, putting his hand on my shoulder, whispered: "You must genuflect on both knees, not merely one, otherwise God will judge you." Mindful of this warning, from that time on I always genuflected on both knees (*Dok.* I).

In Pabianicé, Francis and Raymond made their first Communion together, the former 13 years old, the latter 11 (A. Kubiak, *Dok.* I). Raymond "served Holy Mass from his earliest years" (F. Pisalski, *Pos.*, p. 154), most probably with his brothers. Raymond was the most devout of the three. "His faith and piety set him apart from all the other boys, even his brothers" (A. Zalewski, *Pos.*, p. 530). "He was always eager to attend church" and "like his mother preferred to remain in church to pray." Of Marianna Kolbe, it was said that "in the event she cannot be found at home, look for her in church" (F. Langer, *Pos.*, pp. 476ff.).

In the Church of Saint Matthew, Pabianicé, there are two Marian side altars: one dedicated to Our Lady, Consoler of the Afflicted, and the other to Our Lady of Victory. Near one of these two altars, probably the second, Raymond had the vision of the two crowns recounted by his mother (in the letter to Niepokalanów, October 12, 1941). We can surmise that during his visits to church, Raymond prayed to Jesus in the Blessed Sacrament in a childlike way to be chaste and to be a martyr. It was a reason for wonderment that someone so "joyful and vivacious by nature, . . . full of joy . . . who would have wished, like Saint Francis, to speak with the birds", as he confided to a neighbor in church, Francis Pisalski, "should have been so recollected, full of piety and absorbed in prayer" (*Pos.*, p. 154).

These details from Saint Maximilian's childhood explain, in great part, his later devotion to the Eucharist and are a proof of how great an influence the example of his holy parents had on him.

At Lwów

In 1907, Raymond left for Lwów, where he studied in the minor seminary of the Conventual Franciscans, then made his novitiate year of probation, followed by religious profession in 1911. In the Franciscan environment, his devotion to the Eucharist grew.

His fellow seminarian Father Anselm Kubit recounts:

In the minor seminary, careful attention was given to religious formation. Every day at 6 A.M. we attended Mass. After dinner we made a visit in church, reciting or singing a hymn in honor of the Eucharist. In the evening, after study, we gathered for night prayer and examination of conscience, with some additional prayer proper to the liturgical season. For religious festivities, we assembled in the choir of the church, where enthroned over the high altar was the lovely painting of the Immaculate in the style of Murillo. We went to confession every one or two months, and after each confession we received communion once, since the decree of Saint Pius X in 1905 had not yet gone into effect (*Miles* 15 [1979]: 139).

Another seminarian from the years 1908 to 1909, Reverend Ladislaus Dubaniowski, recounts:

The Servant of God, at the time of our acquaintance, was distinguished among his fellows for his profound faith, shown by exceptional diligence in attending religious exercises, in his piety, in the recitation of the Rosary, in the adoration of the Blessed Sacrament. In church, he knelt in the first choir stall so as to avoid being distracted by his fellows, but with the result that his ardent piety became plain to all. He was a model for us to imitate and was held by us in great esteem. His zeal was not a passing fad, but a permanent characteristic. . . . His great love for God was particularly evident during liturgical ceremonies. All of these he carried out with the greatest exactitude, devoutly, and with recollection. All his gestures and words allowed one to see how deeply he felt and loved the mysteries of faith. He served

Mass willingly, without haste and without slurring the words, which he pronounced in a clear voice. Among the boys he stood out as a model server (*Pos.*, pp. 370ff.).

Raymond Kolbe, according to Father Felix Wilk, "performed the religious exercises with recollection, attention and devotion, without thereby setting himself apart from his fellows. One thing alone stands out in my memory: during a free period I found Raymond in his room, on his knees before the Crucifix and rapt in prayer" (*Pos.*, p. 161).

Still more, in the novitiate, recounts Father Anselm Kubit,

> he understood and absorbed this truth that he lived for God and for his glory, namely, that above all he should give him glory with his own life and that his work should be undertaken with this motive. Hence, with all his heart he dedicated himself to this. His prayers were fervent, particularly after Holy Communion, which at that time we had begun to receive daily. His thanksgivings were heartfelt and vibrant. He knelt without leaning on the pew, with his eyes closed and his face radiant with joy and supernatural peace.
>
> We admired his composure and recollection when assisting at Mass or participating in choir for the recitation of the Breviary.

After religious profession, there still remained a year to complete the study of the humanities, but he did not decrease his "novitiate high flying" (*Miles* 15 [1979]: 147; *Dok.* II, 1, p. 128).

The religious and sacerdotal vocation of Father Maximilian (the name Raymond took at the beginning of the novitiate) was particularly endangered by his patriotism, inclining him to military service in the cause of freeing Poland from a century-old enslavement. Before the altar of the Immaculate, he promised to fight for her. In time he came to understand, principally at her altar, that our Lady was inspiring him to engage in spiritual warfare. He thanked God for having made him "unmask all the tricks of the devil" (*SK* I, 24, p. 41).

At Rome

The years 1912 to 1919 saw Saint Maximilian resident in Rome at the International Seraphic College of the Conventual Franciscans (in Via S. Teodoro, near the Roman Forum), first as a student of philosophy at the Gregorian University and then of theology at the Faculty of Saint Bonaventure attached to the college. In this period, his piety, including the eucharistic, matured.

The most beautiful testimonial to Father Kolbe as someone in love with the Eucharist comes from his closest friend, Father Joseph Pal. He states:

> Love for Jesus in the Blessed Sacrament and love for our Lady touched his pious heart at its very roots. He was enrolled for perpetual adoration at the Monastery of the French Sisters (Adorers) outside Porta Pia. Because both of us were somewhat sickly, with the permission of Father Rector, we took walks alone. Our objective was to visit churches where

there was exposition of the Blessed Sacrament, especially at the Church of the Sacred Heart near the Quirinal, where perpetual adoration was maintained by the French Sisters. In the College, he visited the Blessed Sacrament every hour. After each class or at the end of recreation he visited Jesus in the tabernacle, and in the evening almost always was the last in chapel. From the time he was ordained a priest, he celebrated Mass every day with a maximum of recollection and devotion. One could see in his face how completely absorbed he was in the supernatural world (*Pos.*, pp. 820ff.; *Dok.* II, 1, p. 205).

All of his companions testify that he showed a great and living faith in the Most Blessed Sacrament of the Eucharist (e.g., Fr. John Ossana, *Pos.*, p. 29; Fr. Dominic Stella, *Pos.*, p. 37), and that "he often made private visits to the Blessed Sacrament in addition to those with the community" (Fr. Quiricus Pignalberi, *Pos.*, p. 46). "In entering church or chapel, as he approached the Blessed Sacrament altar, he knelt ordinarily on the floor, not on a kneeler, made a profound and prolonged bow and then remained still" (Fr. John Ossana, *Pos.*, p. 29). Father George Montico attests that as sacristan he often passed through the chapel of the college late at night and found him alone, in the dark, in a posture of devotion. "The Blessed Sacrament", he concludes, "acted on him like a genuine magnet" (*Pos.*, p. 284). "I, too," relates the other sacristan, Father Cyril Kita, "noticed that his face was flushed when he prayed. This indicated that he prayed fervently. I thought I was seeing Saint Stanislaus Kostka himself, with whom he shared a partial, physical resemblance" (*Pos.*, p. 19).

Father Kolbe enrolled in the aforementioned perpetual adoration "to make reparation for the insults done to the Lord" (Fr. Joseph Pal, *Pos.*, p. 824). He was very sensitive about such things. "On hearing any blasphemy," attests Father Andrew Eccher, "he sought at once to make careful reparation, reciting ejaculations or visiting a church and exhorting us, his companions, to do likewise" (*Pos.*, p. 255).

Another eloquent testimonial is that of Monsignor Joseph Palatucci (Bishop of Campania): "I saw Father Kolbe in chapel during Mass, and also at all his other devotional exercises, so composed and reverent, as to reveal in him not only a deep faith in Jesus in the Blessed Sacrament, but throughout his life a spirit preeminently eucharistic" (*Pos.*, p. 62).

The resolutions that at this time he formed during his devotional exercises throw light on the state of his soul during adoration. Already during the 1912 retreat, he encouraged himself to make frequent visits: "Is Jesus happy to dwell under the same roof with you, for you? Go, pay Him a visit" (*SK* II, 962, p. 617); on another occasion he wrote: "Seek there light and strength" (*SK* II, 964, p. 630). On the one hand, he avoided a "lazy casualness", a kind of "excessive familiarity with God in the Blessed Sacrament" (*SK* II, 965, p. 632), and on the other, human respect, seeking to make a "sincere visit to the Blessed Sacrament" (*SK* II, 987 I, p. 722). "Do not be ashamed of your convictions. . . . When you kneel before the altar, do so in such wise that it is evident you are before Him before whom you kneel" (*SK* II, 969, p. 649). During visits, he performed three acts he once listed thus: "Entrust yourself with the Lord in all, thank Him, pray to Him" (*SK* II, 962, p. 611). Worthy of note is his resolution of 1918: "During visits to the Blessed Sacrament, unite yourself to sacrifices of the Mass being celebrated throughout the world" (*SK* II, 987 D, p. 696), to which he added: "Suffer in union with the sufferings of Jesus" (ibid.).

Without doubt, during his adoration in the chapel of the college, Saint Maximilian often derived inspiration for his eucharistic colloquies from the large artistic painting above the altar of the Blessed Sacrament and from the nearby statue of the Immaculate of Lourdes. In the painting was depicted the Sacred Heart of Jesus directing the attention of Saint Margaret Mary Alacoque to Saint Francis of Assisi, saying: "Behold the Saint nearest to my divine Heart." The young Polish Franciscan prodded himself to imitate his Seraphic Patriarch in the love of Jesus and to spread the Kingdom of His Sacred Heart as the Poverello did in the Middle Ages. Deepening as well the devotion of Saint Francis and his order to the Immaculate, he became convinced that "the more one promoted love for the Immaculate, the greater the number of souls one would gain for Her and through Her for the Sacred Heart of Jesus. . . . Such a person shows the greatest love, a practical love for this Sacred Heart, and is united to Him in the highest degree" (*SK* III, 1094, p. 212). From the meditations of Father Kolbe in the chapel of the Seraphic

College, Rome, came the inspiration for the Militia of the Immaculate.

In Niepokalanów

The first building erected in Niepokalanów by Saint Maximilian was the chapel, poorer than the Portiuncula, later to serve as the heart for all the spiritual activities of that immense friary. With what joy in November of 1927 Father Kolbe received permission from Cardinal Alexander Kakowski, archbishop of Warsaw, to celebrate Mass there and to reserve the Blessed Sacrament (*Dok.* II, 1, p. 299). Here, without doubt, was revealed, perhaps most clearly, the eucharistic piety of the founder of the MI. Here were verified to the fullest his statements concerning the fruitfulness of loving encounter with Jesus in the Blessed Sacrament for personal sanctification and for the apostolate.

Reverend Vladimir Obidzinski, the local pastor, attests:

> In all his work, for the development of the friary and for the souls of the Brothers and of all the faithful, he was motivated by the love of God. The modest wooden chapel at Niepokalanów, the services held there, breathed the love of God. Father Kolbe initiated there on the first Fridays of the month entire days of adoration, a practice continued to the present day. The parishioners told me that, on seeing Father Kolbe at the altar, they sensed he lived by the love of God (*Pos.*, p. 129).

Unanimous is the verdict of the friars of Niepokalanów on the unlimited faith and love of their founder for the Eucharist. We have already learned their opinions about his customary manner of celebrating holy Mass; hence it suffices now to examine a few of their testimonials, and those of others, in regard to his practice of adoring Jesus in the Blessed Sacrament.

Father Kolbe often went to chapel to adore the most Blessed Sacrament and encouraged the friars to do likewise. He called such visits "audiences with the great King" (*Dok.* II, 1, p. 153). Brother Luke Kuzba attests:

> Repeatedly throughout the course of the day, he visited Jesus in the tabernacle. He said that there is our strength, there the source of our sanctification. . . . When he was observed there during adoration of the All-Holy, it was not possible to turn one's glance away from his figure, so fascinating it was. During adoration he was ordinarily seen kneeling without support of any kind, just before the steps of the altar (*Pos.*, p. 148).

"He kept his hands under his capuche, and his entire personal composure expressed a profound respect for and the recollected understanding" of the eucharistic mystery, another witness adds (Br. Lawrence Podwapinski, *Pos.*, p. 430). He was so absorbed in prayer, wholly directed to the tabernacle, that he seemed not to notice anyone beside him and that "it was necessary to nudge him first, to inform him of urgent business to be attended to" (Br. Damian Klunejko, *Dok.* II, 1, p. 106). Then, without protest, he would go wherever obedience or love of neighbor called him.

"When for the first time, in 1929," recalls Father Anselm Kubit, "I visited Niepokalanów, I entered the original small, low chapel. Shortly after, Father Maximilian entered in a hurry, did not notice that someone else was also present in the corner, and made adoration with such ardor, with such recollection that this unusual sight made my whole body tremble" (*Dok*. II, 1, p. 135).

Only during the war could Father Kolbe realize his lifelong dream: daily adoration of the most Blessed Sacrament. Brother Benedict Mieczkowski recounts:

> Immediately after his return from prison [1939], Father Maximilian introduced adoration of the most Blessed Sacrament throughout the entire day. He regarded this as the most efficacious means for meeting the needs of Niepokalanów and of his country. He announced this in the refectory and ordered me to assign groups of friars from each work sector to take turns adoring for a half-hour each. On each turn, there were several friars. In this way, each, including Father Maximilian, had his own time of adoration each day. Great care and attention were given to this activity. Often, in the early days, he himself would check and remind the brothers of this commitment, so that they would come to realize it as a duty and consider it of vital importance. But above all, he encouraged us with his example, more than once going to the chapel to take the place of someone absent. When he did not feel well, he would get his cane and, leaning on it, would take his

place in the chapel for the period of adoration assigned him immediately after the afternoon rest, sometime between 3 and 4 P.M. (*Dok.* II, 2, p. 280).

It made him happy to see a group of his friars around the altar in adoration. When he showed guests about Niepokalanów, at times Germans from the highest ranks of society, he either began or ended the visit in the chapel to greet, as he explained, the Master of the house (Br. Stephan Nowicki, *Dok.* II, 1, p. 201). Indicating the religious adoring the most Blessed Sacrament, he would say: "There is the most important work department in the friary" (Br. Luke Kuzba, *Dok.* II, 1, p. 143; Br. John Bednarski, *Dok.* II, 2, p. 47).

This adoration was carried out simply before the tabernacle, except on first Fridays of the month when the Blessed Sacrament was exposed in a monstrance, and only during the day, not at night. Notwithstanding the ardent desire of the saint to have perpetual adoration, he took account of the exhaustion of the friars after a hard day's work. At times, however, he would give an individual permission for nocturnal adoration. Brother Ives Achtelik recalls:

> I know some friars who every Thursday asked permission to make the "holy hour" from 11 P.M. to midnight, and to whom he always gave permission willingly. I, too, received this permission from time to time, and also with an intention to be present during the adoration. On such occasions, he would say that he would gladly have participated in these nightly holy hours, but obedience required him to

retire at 9 P.M., an hour before the rest (*Dok.* II, 1, p. 2).

As in Niepokalanów, so elsewhere, Father Kolbe conducted himself, edifying all by his eucharistic devotion. "The Servant of God", Reverend Obidzinski tells us, "preached often during retreats organized for my parishioners at Pawłowice. When not preaching or hearing confessions, he always went to church to make a quarter-hour of adoration before the Blessed Sacrament. Even during cloudbursts he did not fail to visit the church for customary adoration" (*Pos.*, p. 406). "More than once," recounts Sister Felicity Sulatycka, "I saw the Servant of God rapt in profound adoration both at Zakopane and in our chapel at Szymanów" (*Pos.*, p. 337). When he adored Jesus in the tabernacle, states Sister Adele Nowak, "at times he seemed to me not to be on this earth" (*Rel.*, p. 91). "Father", remarked another sister jokingly, "will probably wear a hole in the kneeler, he stays there so long" (Sr. Anna Kilian, *Rel.*, p. 54).

While adoring Jesus in the Blessed Sacrament in the "old chapel" at Niepokalanów, Father Kolbe at times raised his eyes to the statue of the Immaculate and the painting of the Sacred Heart of Jesus above the altar. Thus, his zeal to achieve the goal of the MI was stimulated. How inspiring were his conferences after these visits! For example, on December 15, 1936, he said:

> We must launch a general offensive on the occasion of the first decade of Niepokalanów. Before all else, we must conquer our own souls for the Immaculate

and through Her for the Sacred Heart of Jesus. This is the most important bastion to storm. At the same time, we must conquer all of Niepokalanów, helping each other in the task. Finally, I say it trembling, of over two billion souls, only a very small part honor and serve the Immaculate, and the rest do not know Her, do not know Her Son, or have forgotten them. We must bring all these to the feet of the Immaculate. We must conquer the world for the Immaculate, and through Her for the Sweet Heart of Jesus, and this as soon as possible! So then, dear sons, to the attack, on the offensive! (*CK,* December 15, 1936).

In Japan

On February 26, 1930, Saint Maximilian celebrated Mass in the "old chapel" of Niepokalanów "according to the intentions of the Immaculate", i.e., to conquer the world through her for the Sacred Heart of Jesus; it was his last homage to the Blessed Sacrament before leaving for the Far East. During the sea voyage, at the hour of adoration in common in Niepokalanów, he united himself spiritually to Jesus in the Blessed Sacrament with his heart, adoring Him from afar (Br. Hilary Lysakowski, *Dok*. II, 1, p. 152). He celebrated Mass on board ship or in churches of port cities.

At Nagasaki, Father Kolbe, as Father Mieczislaus Mirochna, his disciple from 1930, attests,

> very often visited the Blessed Sacrament. In any difficulty, he ran to Jesus in the Blessed Sacrament to seek the necessary strength. He desired to work by

means of perpetual adoration of the Blessed Sacrament. He explained that veneration of the Blessed Virgin Mary was necessary to bring us to the worship of the Savior Jesus Christ. In the celebration of Mass, his devotion was evident to all who attended: his eyes were fixed on the Host. Each day he visited the Blessed Sacrament more than ten times with great devotion. He took care to celebrate feast days worthily (*Pos.*, p. 191).

During the first year, the Polish missionaries resided in the Oura quarter near the cathedral, where they held religious services. "When our little missionary group grew larger [in March 1931]," recounts Brother Romuald Mrozinski, "Bishop Hayasaka allowed us to celebrate Mass in our own house, but without permission to reserve the Blessed Sacrament (because of the structural weakness of the house). Hence, we often visited the Cathedral (3 minutes on foot) to adore the Blessed Sacrament. We also attended Sunday benediction and May devotions" (*Dok.* II, 2, p. 300). But even this short distance was not easy for Father Kolbe. In November 1930, he confided to his provincial: "We must, notwithstanding the fall rains and cold wind, climb the hill every day, then some sixty steps to the parish church for Holy Mass", and "my lungs" feel it (*SK* I, 292, p. 441).

At Mugenzai no Sono, however, the Eucharist was always reserved in the chapel. Modest, like that of Niepokalanów, this chapel expressed in equal measure the heart of Father Kolbe. Brother Henry Borodziej, his collaborator, writes:

We commonly read of the saints how they spent long hours in prayer. Our Father Maximilian, unfortunately, did not have time for long prayers. After reciting the prescribed religious prayers, he was immersed in editorial duties. But on any possible occasion he would visit chapel for a moment, usually two or three minutes, to be with Jesus in the Blessed Sacrament. This was his style of life, and hence worthy of being recorded (*Dok.* II, 2, p. 57).

When teaching clerics, whether in the major seminary of the diocese or in that of the order, after each class, he visited the cathedral or his own chapel and encouraged his students to do likewise. "When he taught us theology," recalls Father Mirochna, "each hour he visited the Blessed Sacrament with us" (*Pos.*, p. 710). In Mugenzai no Sono, where two Polish and three Japanese clerics were studying, these together with their professor, "during the break between classes would take a stroll on a path near the chapel; at the end of the stroll, Father Kolbe, without entering the chapel, so as not to have to take off his shoes according to Japanese custom, would kneel with the others on the threshold for a short prayer" (*Dok.* II, 2, p. 57).

The example of Saint Maximilian attracted many. "The devotion of the Servant of God to the Blessed Sacrament", attests Father Cornelius Czupryk, guardian of Mugenzai no Sono between 1933 and 1936, "was exceptional. He was accustomed often to visit the Blessed Sacrament both at night as well as during the day. He celebrated Holy Mass with great piety and recollection. There was nothing eccentric about this piety" (*Pos.*, p. 108). "Before the Blessed Sacrament," adds Brother Gerard Radziewicz, "he was always recollected and full of reverence" (*Pos.*, p. 718). "During Holy Mass," says Brother Romuald Mrozinski, "his face would become radiant: love burned brightly in him." So too, during adoration of Jesus in the Blessed Sacrament, his comportment was always humble and "his eyes were aflame with zeal" (*Dok.* II, 1, p. 197).

The Japanese were impressed and edified by the eucharistic devotion of Father Kolbe. Here are some testimonials from his students: "His comportment before the Blessed Sacrament clearly demonstrates his faith in the Real Presence of Jesus therein. Often, even if only briefly, he made the most devout visits to the Blessed Eucharist" (Rev. M. Iwanga Shizuo, *Pos.*, p. 286). "In the presence of the Blessed Sacrament his face showed that he almost really saw the living Christ" (Rev. G. Makajima Manri, *Pos.*, p. 201). Professor Paul Nagai recalls that Father Kolbe "often visited the Blessed Sacrament and exhorted others to do likewise" (*Pos.*, p. 195). Bishop Januarius Hayasaka attests: "He seems to have had a strong faith in the holy Eucharist. Ordinarily, before receiving appointments, he would remain in meditation before the Blessed Sacrament" (*Pos.*, p. 198). And Brother Sergius Pesiek of Nagasaki recalls: "In summertime, when it was particularly hot, we would often go to the seashore to bathe. Usually we would take a small boat to Joyima; there was also a church we visited to adore the Blessed Sacrament" (*Dok.* II, 2, p. 408).

Almost the first thing discovered on Father Kolbe's arrival in Japan, on his first day near the Cathedral of Nagasaki, "was a large statue of our Lady . . . that seemed to beckon him into church" (*SK* III, 1182, p. 394). And so each day thereafter, for nearly a year, when he lived in the Oura quarter, and later when he would go to teach in the diocesan seminary, she seemed to beckon him into church. And in he always went, adoring Jesus in the Blessed Sacrament and strengthening himself spiritually so as to cope with the many problems in the life of a missionary. Thanks to the Eucharist alone, Saint Maximilian was able to persevere in Japan and produce much fruit by his missionary activity.

In the Concentration Camps

During the war as well, although for many months Saint Maximilian was separated from the altar of the Lord, the Eucharist constituted his strength. During the German invasion of September 1939, Saint Maximilian, "while celebrating Mass one day," recounts Brother John Bednarski, "gave us Communion several times so as to consume all the consecrated hosts, because he feared profanation by German soldiers. Afterward, in the detention camp, we said among ourselves that it was probably in view of three months compulsory fast from the bread of angels that we had earlier received so abundant a eucharistic banquet from Father Kolbe" (*Dok.* II, 2, p. 23).

In fact, during his first deportation with some thirty friars to the internment camps at Lamsdorf,

Amtitz, and Ostrzeszów, Father Kolbe could not celebrate Mass. Only on the last day of imprisonment, December 8, in Ostrzeszów, Brother Cyprian Grodski recalls with emotion:

> Father Maximilian had prepared for us a spiritual banquet. Before the feast of the Immaculate Conception, we made a retreat of eight days, listening to four conferences of Father Pius Bartoski, with an introductory and concluding conference by Father Kolbe. The commandant of the camp was a Protestant minister. On occasion, Father Kolbe had conversation with him and was greatly respected by him. On the vigil of the Immaculate Conception, the commandant himself, at the request of Father Kolbe, went to the local [Catholic] pastor, asking him to bring Communion to the religious. "He [the Protestant minister] can also serve the cause of the Immaculate", declared Father Kolbe. On the day of the feast, at 5 A.M., the Blessed Sacrament arrived in camp. In a dark room illumined by a few candles, the friars, recollected, received Communion about the large tissue-paper cross on the wall. So too, the Christians of the first centuries received Communion in the catacombs. What a moving scene! (*Dok.* II, 1, p. 78).

Perhaps this hunger for the Eucharist, experienced in these camps, moved Saint Maximilian, immediately on his return to Niepokalanów, to introduce permanent daily adoration of the Blessed Sacrament, as described above (cf. pp. 109–11).

It is not known whether Father Kolbe even once succeeded in celebrating Holy Mass in Pawiak prison,

Warsaw, where he was held from February 17 to May 28, 1941. Leon Wanat in his book *Kartki z Pawiaka* [Letters from Pawiak, Warsaw, 1978] writes: "Right from the start of the occupation, the Polish guards in Pawiak allowed medals and other articles necessary for priests, such as missals, stoles, hosts, to be brought in" (p. 17). From another source, we learn that "before Easter, Father Kolbe organized a retreat for the personnel of the library where the young intellectuals of Warsaw worked" (Rev. Joseph Kopczewski, *Zez.*, p. 31). It is possible that on occasion the saint may have celebrated Mass in secret, or at least have distributed consecrated hosts sometimes brought into Pawiak (cf. *Kartki*, p. 204).

In the concentration camp of Oświęcim, it was impossible, especially in 1941, to celebrate Mass. Such is the opinion of ex-prisoners. Only one, Henry Sienkiewicz, recalls: "On one occasion I brought a package of hosts, which I had received from Mrs. Kania, to the Servant of God. Father Maximilian Kolbe— this I know—twice celebrated Holy Mass between cell blocks in the greatest secrecy and about 30 of the prisoners attended and all received Holy Communion from the hands of the Servant of God" (*Pos.*, p. 458). But whether the service referred to in this testimony was in fact a Mass is open to question. It is possible that the celebration was but the distribution of the consecrated hosts, mentioned above, that had been smuggled into the concentration camp from without. Ladislaus Lewkowicz recounts that sometimes, with a few prisoners, he would receive Communion from Father Kolbe (*Zez.*, pp. 36ff.).

Marianna Kolbe, who, more than anyone else, understood the eucharistic devotion of her son, stated after his death: "My greatest sorrow was the knowledge that he remained deprived of Holy Mass and Communion so long" (Letter to Niepokalanów, October 12, 1941).

In spite of that, the saint forced himself constantly to turn his mind, and those of the prisoners, toward God, particularly on Sunday, the Lord's day. "During his free time," states Alexander Dziuba,

> in the evening and on Sunday afternoons, the Servant of God would assemble trusted persons. These small groups changed often. He took advantage of these meetings to engage in discussion of religious questions, to raise our spirits, and to strengthen us in face of the fear of death. During these meetings we often prayed and some would confess to him (*Pos.*, p. 455).

> It is a fact that at times, after confession, we desired to receive Holy Communion, but this was not possible, since, at that time, it was not permitted to celebrate Holy Mass in the camp. The Servant of God, desiring to symbolize Holy Communion for us in some way, would take his own bread, bless it, and give a piece to each of us (*Pos.*, p. 458).

A record exists of a talk Father Kolbe gave on the feast of Corpus Christi, in June of 1941. Mieczislaus Koscielniak, a Polish artist, recounts:

> On this day, the camp could relax for a few hours, since the SS had received permission to go to town and the bosses had given us a bit of peace.

After the so-called dinner, I was invited between blocks 18 and 19 where several persons had gathered, among whom were several priests. . . . We sat on the bricks and beams being readied for the erection of a new block. Our colleague Kolbe began to speak *sotto voce*. He spoke of the Feast of Corpus Christi, of the great and omnipotent God, and of our sufferings by which He was trying to make us ready for a better life. He encouraged us to persevere and to be brave. . . . Strengthened by this spirit, we returned to our blocks. No, we will not give up, we said, we will surely persevere; they will not succeed in destroying the Polish soul in us by terror. And if we must die, we will die without shame and without fear, submitting ourselves to the judgment of God: so Father Maximilian Kolbe, Franciscan, great priest, spoke to us (*Zez.*, p. 34).

Without doubt, the saint, above all when he could not celebrate Mass, practiced spiritual communion. While still a young seminarian, he wrote: "At times, spiritual communion brings the same graces as sacramental" (*SK* II, 968, p. 647). He resolved to engage "more often in spiritual communion, at least once every quarter hour" (*SK* II, 987 I, p. 720). In 1912, during retreat, he noted: "When you have no time to go to Jesus, and temptations assail you, and you do not know what to do, hold the Cross to your chest, kiss His holy wounds, and He will support you" (*SK* II, 962, p. 618). In Oświęcim, at the request of Father Kolbe, the artist Koscielniak drew two small pencil sketches: one of Christ and one of our Lady, which the Servant of

God always carried on his person (cf. *Pos.*, p. 354). These he used for those loving colloquies once conducted in churches and chapels. To Reverend Conrad Szweda, Father Kolbe confided what he had often experienced: "When their hands, one of Christ and one of Mary most holy, support you, you can go on, even in the dark, with the certainty that no evil will overtake you, as a child on the shoulders of its parents" (*Pos.*, p. 638).

After all that has been said of the eucharistic devotion and life of Saint Maximilian Mary, on the basis of eyewitness evidence, it is possible to understand even better his repeated assertions that the closer we are to the Immaculate, the closer we approach her divine Son. "Love the Immaculate with all your heart", he wrote in 1937 to one of his confreres [Brother Felicissimus Sztyk]; "fly often to Her by means of ejaculations, or simply with the thought of Her, and She will teach you how to return to Jesus a love without measure for the love which He showed on the Cross and in the most Blessed Sacrament of the altar" (*SK* II, 715, pp. 308–9).

The statements of two brothers of Niepokalanów accurately summarize all these testimonials: "The Immaculate fascinated the heart of Father Maximilian. She herself, as no one else could, instilled in him his ardent love for Jesus, because, as he himself stressed, through Her it is possible, quickly and securely, to find Jesus and love Him in the manner worthy of Him" (Br. John Bednarski, *Dok.* II, 2, p. 47). "As a true Mother, the Immaculate taught

Her perfect knight how to worship the King of love with genuine adoration, and initiated him into the secret of intimate union with Jesus" (Br. Benedict Mieczkowski, *Dok.* II, 2, p. 281).

IV

THE MILITIA OF THE IMMACULATE AND THE EUCHARIST

Cities of the Immaculate (Niepokalanóws) consecrated totally to the Immaculate and to her cause, above all honor the Eucharist, live by the Eucharist, find in the Eucharist the principal source for their apostolate, and hope to unite the whole world as one family about the standard of the Eucharist and Mary. This ideal is pursued by the entire Militia of the Immaculate. Every knight knows that in this way he imitates his founder, Saint Maximilian Mary Kolbe, that great devotee of the Eucharist. In him—by reason of his total consecration to the Mother of Jesus—"the love of Jesus in the Blessed Sacrament touched his pious heart at its very roots" (Fr. Joseph Pal, *Pos.*, p. 820).

The Eucharist—God with Us

Contemplating the mystery of the Eucharist, Father Kolbe was convinced—and this conviction inspired the MI—that the most Blessed Sacrament is the richest of divine treasures on earth, the source for the sanctification of souls and for the conversion of the world, and thus the most efficacious means for attaining the goals of the MI.

Saint Maximilian based his faith in the Eucharist on the gospel and on the teaching of the Church. In an article entitled *"Corpus Domini"* (Body of the Lord) published in 1924 in *Rycerz Niepokalanej* and occasioned by a blasphemy perpetrated at Grodno by a group of drunken non-Catholics on the Feast of Corpus Christi, he assembled the gospel proofs for the dogma of the Blessed Sacrament.

In the Gospel of Saint John, an eyewitness, is found the promise made to the people at Capernaum after the multiplication of the loaves to give us as food His own flesh and His own blood. "Amen, amen, I say to you: if you do not eat of the flesh of the Son of man and do not drink of His blood, you shall not have life in you." Life here means life to the full, "life everlasting". "For my flesh is food indeed and my blood drink indeed. Who eats of my flesh and drinks of my blood, remains in me and I in him"; so too he "shall live because of me" (Jn 6:51–60).

A year later, at Jerusalem in the Upper Room, during the Last Supper with the apostles, Jesus fulfilled this promise. "While they were at supper," recounts Saint Matthew, who was present, "Jesus took bread, blessed and broke it, and gave it to His disciples: 'Take and eat; this is my body.' And taking a cup, he gave thanks and gave it to them, saying: 'All of you drink of this; for this is my blood of the new covenant, which is being shed for many unto the forgiveness of sins'" (Mt 26:26–28). And He added, as Saint Luke (22:19) and Saint Paul (1 Cor 11:24–25) attest: "Do this in memory of me."

"And from that moment," concludes Father Kolbe, recalling the bimillenary practice of the Church, "the sacrifice of the Holy Mass made its appearance on the earth. Ever more often, ever more widespread. At first underground in the catacombs, later in an ever-growing number of churches." Every "priest, a successor of the Apostles," obedient to the command of the God-Man, repeats at Mass, "in His memory the moving scene of the Last Supper": the bread becomes "the living Body of Christ" and the wine "His most precious Blood". Christ remains really present under the consecrated species, also after the Mass. He dwells in tabernacles, and on the solemnity of Corpus Christi during the eucharistic procession, "He, the Creator of heaven and of earth and the Redeemer of souls" goes out "upon the streets and roads of His children, carried in the hands of the priest" (*SK* III, 1059, pp. 133–35).

Saint Maximilian desired to write a book on the teaching of the Church with a chapter entitled "Dogma: The Most Blessed Sacrament" (*SK* III, 1270, p. 648), perhaps eventually to be published as a booklet. He wished to write of dogma "in a popular, lively style, illustrating the doctrine with miracles attested by competent witnesses (for example, bearing on the Eucharist)" (Alph., p. 41). The constant demands of the apostolate did not permit him to write such a work. But in the material for a book on the Immaculate, we find the description of the apparition of our Lady to Alphonse Ratisbonne in the

Church of Sant'Andrea delle Fratte, Rome, together with an account of a moral miracle bearing on the Eucharist. In an instant, this unbelieving Jew, without hearing so much as a word from the all holy Virgin, understood the entire Catholic Faith, including the truth about the Eucharist.

"The Catholic Faith", recounts Mr. de Bussieres, a friend of Ratisbonne and witness of his conversion, "welled up from his heart, as a rare perfume from its container, unable to be kept sealed within. He spoke of the Real Presence (of Jesus in the Blessed Sacrament), as a man who believes in it with all the strength of his soul, nay, rather as a man who has experienced it." Shortly thereafter, between the Basilicas of Saint Mary Major and Saint Peter, he was filled by an indescribable, ecstatic rapture.

> "Oh," he said to me, grasping my hands, "now I understand the love of Catholics for their churches and the devotion which impels them to decorate and embellish them! . . . This is no longer earth, but almost paradise." Before the altar of the Blessed Sacrament, the *Real Presence* of the divinity overwhelmed him to such a point that he visited less often and would often leave at once, so awesome it seemed to him to remain in the presence of the living God with the stain of original sin! (He was not yet baptized.) And he would flee to a chapel of the all holy Virgin (*SK* III, 1315, p. 733).

Saint Maximilian was deeply touched by the real presence of Jesus, the God-Man, under the eucharistic species. Before the Blessed Sacrament altar, he acted as though he saw the Savior. "God dwells in our midst", he exclaimed, "in the Blessed Sacrament of the altar" (*SK* III, 1088, p. 195). "He remains among us until the end of the world. He dwells on so many altars, though so often offended and profaned" (*CK*, April 14, 1938). But even more, the founder of the MI was fascinated by the fact that Jesus in the sacrament gives Himself to us as food. Once he went so far as to say: "The culmination of the Mass is not the consecration, but Communion" (*CK*, March 10, 1940). With his heart full of gratitude, he said to Jesus: "You come to me and unite yourself intimately to me under the form of nourishment. Your blood now runs in mine, your soul, Incarnate God, compenetrates mine, giving it courage and support. What miracles! Who would ever have imagined such!" (*SK* III, 1145, p. 326). "If angels could be jealous of men," Father Kolbe was in the habit of saying, "they would be so for one reason: Holy Communion" (*CK*, December 18, 1938).

What grace is given to man and what dignity his to be able to attend holy Mass and receive holy Communion! "It is accessible to all, without exception", said Saint Maximilian to his confreres. "The time during which Jesus abides in us under the sacramental species is the most precious of the entire day." Not only the body but "the soul then becomes a living tabernacle, indeed something even more. At that time, the soul of Jesus unites itself with our soul and becomes the soul of our soul. We cannot understand all this, but can only perceive the effects" (*CK*, March 10, 1940). How many the graces one can receive, "if the very Giver of graces arrives" (*CK*, March 16, 1938).

What good fortune for religious to be able to dwell with Jesus in the Blessed Sacrament under the same roof, or very near, and attend holy Mass every day, to go whenever they wish to their "elder Brother and Spouse of their souls present in the Eucharist" (*SK* III, 1239, p. 553). "At times we meet persons", Father Kolbe told his confreres in Niepokalanów, "who cannot imagine what religious life might be; they think it is a prison. They neither know nor experience the joy which the Sacraments give", above all daily Communion, the happiness "of living in union with God, the font of happiness. Should someone propose to exchange this for a great quantity of gold, the religious soul would be shocked and astounded" (*CK*, December 18, 1938).

Superabundant Font of Grace

The Second Vatican Council stressed that "in the Blessed Eucharist is contained the entire spiritual treasure of the Church, Christ himself, our Pasch and the living Bread, who through His flesh, quickened and quickening in the Holy Spirit, gives life to men. In such wise these are invited and drawn to offer in union with Him their own work and all creation. Thus, the Eucharist is recognized as the source and summit of all evangelization" (*Presbyterorum ordinis*, no. 5).

Saint Maximilian understood this well. According to him, the Eucharist brings extraordinary blessings for our sanctification and apostolate. In general, he considered prayer as the most efficacious means for realizing the goal of the MI. "God wills", he assures us, "that humble souls, who love him and hence pray to him, govern the world with divine goodness and power, save and sanctify souls and inaugurate in them the reign of divine love" (*SK* III, 1302, p. 707). Our influence on the world "in the natural order depends on our position, work, abilities, circumstances, etc.", but "in the supernatural order, we can influence without measure", precisely through prayer, so that the future of the world depends on hands raised in prayer (*CK*, March 10, 1940). And the summit of prayer is precisely the Mass and within the Mass— holy Communion (ibid.), wherein we receive the Giver of graces. "I can do all things in Him who strengthens me", Saint Maximilian was accustomed to say, citing Saint Paul (Phil 4:13), and he often added "through the Immaculate" (*SK* II, 968, p. 645 and passim). "One Holy Communion alone", observed Father Kolbe during the retreat of 1917, "is sufficient to make me a Saint" (*SK* II, 968, p. 647). From this period as well comes the saying: "Divine office and the Mass, celebrated well, can renew an entire diocese" (*SK* II, 968, p. 647). He was impressed with Saint Pius X, who wished "to renew all in Christ", above all via a renewed eucharistic devotion.

The founder of the MI believed that in the Mass, at Communion, one could ask anything, both for one's own sanctification and for the salvation of one's neighbor. "The Giver of graces Himself comes—we can pray to Him for many things through the Immaculate" (*CK*, February 16, 1938). He is "the font of every truth, of every good and of all happiness" (*SK* III, 1079, p. 168). How long are the lists for the "Memento of the Living" and for that of the dead whom our saint recommended to God in every Mass, praying above all for their spiritual welfare. With that faith, he asked of others a memento at Mass or that they receive Communion according to his missionary intentions and thanked them for such help. To the clerics of Kraków, he wrote from Japan: "Offer Holy Communion, and so doing you will help us much" (*SK* I, 301, p. 463). He thanked the brothers of Niepokalanów in 1930 for the Communions received in his behalf on the occasion of his name day: "May the Immaculate repay all for the Holy Communions, for in the missions such help is absolutely necessary" (*SK* I, 286, p. 430). To render eucharistic prayer more efficacious, he encouraged himself and others "to offer to the Immaculate Holy Communion, as Her property, for purposes pleasing to Her" (*SK* I, 463, p. 858). And he thanked God for the graces received, for he realized that gratitude increases the graces and that in such wise one also respects the character of the Eucharist in view of its etymology (giving thanks). Consistent with his faith in the universal mediation of Mary, he gave particular thanks for the graces granted the Immaculate and encouraged such practice. "It is good to thank the Most Blessed Trinity for the graces given Her. Let us show this gratitude during Communion" (*CK*, November 26, 1938).

Indeed, one Communion alone can make us saints, can effect the conversion of many sinners, but "all depends (also) on our interior dispositions, our preparation" (*SK* II, 968, p. 647). The Eucharist is food to be consumed with a pure heart, purified by frequent confession. Father Kolbe exhorted the members of the MI that "they should approach the table of the Lord with a pure heart. . . . Only a pure soul, in fact, is disposed to receive grace" (*SK* III, 1079, p. 167). Of great importance for the fruitfulness of the Eucharist is the immediate preparation for Mass and thanksgiving afterward, which may and should be anticipated and prolonged through the diligent fulfillment of one's duties, with the desire of bringing joy to the Sacred Heart of Jesus. To receive an abundance of graces at Mass, it is necessary to pray much, above all, after holy Communion (*CK*, January 24, 1933). All this under the maternal guidance of the Immaculate. "Strive as much as you are able to please Jesus as a form of preparation and thanksgiving" (*SK* II, 987 E, p. 698).

Saint Maximilian especially recommended adoration of the Blessed Sacrament. When one believes in the real presence of the God-Man in the tabernacle, when one professes with Father Kolbe: "He is our all" (*SK* II, 987 B, p. 686), one cannot remain indifferent, above all when one dwells near the house of God. Love impels one to visit the Divine Prisoner of love. Another motive is that of reparation for one's own sins and for those of the entire world, particularly on the first Friday of the month, as Jesus himself requested through Saint Margaret Mary Alacoque in

1674. On November 4, 1938 (a first Friday), Father Kolbe told his friars in Niepokalanów: "When a friendship meets indifference as a response, such causes pain. If men of the world, rejected by those whom they loved, take their lives, because unable to bear the sorrow they experience, so too the Most Sacred Heart of Jesus feels great sorrow when His love is rejected." Hence, souls who love Him "strive to make recompense for those others who repay the unlimited love of the divine Heart with ingratitude" so that "at least in part, recompense is made for a rejected love. The soul experiences these graces, and for this even more ardently repays divine love with love" (*CK*, November 4, 1938).

By means of adoration of the most Blessed Sacrament, one can receive many graces for the conversion and sanctification of souls. The MI values this as one of the most important means for achieving its own goals. It made Father Kolbe's heart glad to see many friars often about the altar in adoration, because, as he remarked, "religious formation depends on drawing close to the Lord Jesus, on visiting Him" (*CK*, September 3, 1937). "When I arrived at Niepokalanów," recounts Father Isidore Kozbial, recalling his entrance into the minor seminary in 1929, "Father Maximilian led me, together with my pastor, to the chapel and observed: 'All religious life depends on this'—and pointed to the Most Blessed Sacrament" (*Pos.*, p. 164). So too the fruitfulness of the apostolate depends on adoration.

For many years, Saint Maximilian dreamed of the day when "in the chapel at Niepokalanów Jesus would be exposed day and night in the monstrance and there would be enough friars to adore Him uninterruptedly in turns of two or more" (*SK* I, 354, p. 584), or "at least throughout the entire day" (*SK* I, 454, p. 838), even if without exposition. Recalling in 1938 his design for the church in Niepokalanów, he added with emphasis:

> If half the brothers worked and the other half prayed, this would not be too much (*CK*, March 5, 1938). [At that time there were in Niepokalanów about 570 brothers, not counting fathers and candidates for the priesthood.]
>
> In such wise, the apostolate on behalf of souls in Poland, in the missions and everywhere, would also be enriched by ever more abundant graces (*SK* I, 454, p. 838).
>
> How many blessings the adorers would gain for each copy of the *Rycerz* (in whatever language published). ... And further, how many the graces indispensable for the growth of every work, for every soul consecrated to the Immaculate or who should belong to Her, whether in Niepokalanów or in the MI. I have before my eyes the blessing of the sick with the Blessed Sacrament in the Grotto of the Immaculate at Lourdes. But this is a dream! (*SK* I, 354, p. 584).

This dream, already conceived in 1931, but difficult to realize before the war because of the massive work load, was inaugurated, at least partially (adoration during the day and without exposition in the monstrance), in 1939, immediately after his return from his first imprisonment by the Germans.

"Initially in turns of two", wrote the saint joyfully, "then of four, and now six brothers every half-hour take turns throughout the day; and thus uninterruptedly throughout the entire day there flows a torrent of prayer, the greatest power in the world, capable of transforming us and changing the face of the world" (*SK* II, 895, p. 528). He added: "At the present moment this is the most important activity" (*SK* II, 892, p. 513; *SK* II, 954, pp. 599ff.).

Saint Maximilian encouraged others, especially members of the MI, to adore Jesus in the Blessed Sacrament often, in this way to help the work being conducted under the banner of the Immaculate. He wrote in 1931:

> We have unending woes in both Niepokalanóws; we will have still more. Does it not seem, therefore, the right moment to establish prayer circles and associations of the suffering for the intentions of the MI? How much we would have gained, for example, if sisters, particularly contemplatives, had offered something for the MI: a small part of their sufferings and of their adoration of the Blessed Sacrament (*SK* I, 363, p. 611).

The practice of perpetual adoration of the Blessed Sacrament throughout the entire day, ordinarily without solemn exposition, except on the first Friday of each month, has continued in Niepokalanów to the present day. Marytown in America, however, some years ago introduced perpetual adoration of the Blessed Sacrament exposed in the monstrance day and night, and in which not only religious but laity participate. Eucharistic adoration at Marytown, among other things, is an excellent means for the formation of young members of the MI, known as YMI (Youth Mission for the Immaculate), during their annual monthlong retreat. Marytown also promotes perpetual adoration in parishes and has succeeded in introducing the practice in about 100 of these, to the great spiritual profit of the faithful. The practice originated with Father Cyril Kita, a co-founder of Marytown, who, as a fellow student of Saint Maximilian in Rome, remained deeply impressed by his eucharistic adoration.

The Love of Love through the Immaculate

When we deepen our understanding of the reason for the institution of the Eucharist, we perceive that it "is the fruit of the love of Jesus" (*CK*, June 28, 1936). It seemed that the love Jesus showed on earth from His Incarnation to His sacrifice on Calvary was the last word of His heart. Father Kolbe said to Jesus:

> You, however, did not stop with this, but foreseeing all that would happen across nineteen centuries from the moment of these outpourings of your love to my appearance on earth [January 8, 1894], you desired to make provision even for this! Your heart was not satisfied that I should be nourished only with a memory of your infinite love. You remained in this vale of tears in the most holy and singularly miraculous Sacrament of the Altar

and gave yourself to me "in possession" (*SK* III, 1145, p. 326).

The soul pondering all these marks of love should desire to return love for love (*CK*, June 28, 1936). In fact, "the King of love can be honored only with love" (*CK*, October 27, 1940). To His infinite love, we must reply with a love without limits. "Does not God who remains in the world under the species of bread, who empties Himself to such a degree, merit a limitless love in return? God gives us Himself; we instead have received what we give" and what we can give (*CK*, June 16, 1939). The sacraments, above all the Eucharist, were granted us precisely "in order to gain the strength to overcome all the obstacles blocking our pilgrimage to God, with a love ever more burning, by being conformed to God, in being united with God himself" (*SK* III, 1332, p. 792). "We are reborn in holy Baptism, because it washes away our sins. We are renewed again and again in the sacrament of Penance. We must, so to speak, divinize ourselves and for this we have the most Blessed Sacrament. We receive not only grace, but the Giver of grace Himself, who accomplishes this divinization in the measure he finds our souls disposed for this" (*CK*, March 28, 1937). But we know from experience how weak our preparation is and how imperfect our disposition, even during Communion, and not simply because of our psychosomatic constitution, source of so many distractions and of spiritual dryness, hence not always culpable. At times, our faith is weak; otherwise, with what devotion we would receive holy Communion (*CK*, June 5, 1938). There remains in the soul self-love in the form, for example, of attachments; this is the betrayal of Love and the greatest obstacle to sanctification (*CK*, June 16, 1939; April 24, 1938).

Knowing our human weakness, Jesus "in the love of his divine Heart gives us as mother His own Mother so that we might love Him with Her heart: no longer with our miserable heart, but with Her Immaculate Heart. The love of the Immaculate is the most perfect love with which the creature can love his God" (*CK*, June 28, 1936). "No man or angel loved or loves Jesus as ardently as the Mother of God." Hence, we in the MI "place no limits on love. We want to love the Lord Jesus with Her heart, or rather that She love Him with our heart. We wish precisely that our love for God be that of the Immaculate. So that such in fact occur, we must become Her property and be Hers totally, under every aspect" (*CK*, September 4, 1937). By consecrating ourselves totally to the Immaculate as her instrument, we can take advantage to the maximum of her grace and of her example.

In our eucharistic devotion as well, we must love Love with the Heart of the Immaculate, if we wish our love to be as worthy and pleasing as possible to Jesus. So too, during eucharistic devotion, "we wish to love the Lord Jesus with the heart of the Immaculate, receiving Him and thanking Him with Her acts; thus, even if we should neither feel nor understand it, in fact we will honor the Lord Jesus with Her heart, with Her acts; or to speak more exactly, it will be She who through us loves and praises Jesus. We are but Her instruments" (*CK*, July 5, 1936).

"How must we prepare ourselves for Holy Communion so as to be well disposed and to obtain therein as many graces as possible?" reflected Saint Maximilian at Easter of 1937. He concluded: "Let us give ourselves to the Immaculate. Let us permit Her to prepare us to receive Jesus in Holy Communion. This is the most perfect way and the one most pleasing to our Lord, yielding the greatest fruit" (*CK*, March 28, 1937). So also, in reference to the Eucharist, the founder of the MI returns to this *leitmotiv* of total consecration to the Immaculate, the consecration making one an instrument in her hands. And here he has a very particular reason. With the Incarnation in mind, he asks: "Who, in the first instance, offered Holy Mass? and who received the first Communion? and who was His first tabernacle?" And he replies: "The all holy Mother!" (*CK*, undated). All this Mary did in the most perfect manner possible; hence, Jesus gave her to us as Mother and gave us to her as sons, so that we might find an effective supporter.

To understand this reasoning better, it is necessary to view the entire economy of salvation, as the founder of the MI presents it, in the light of the Immaculate Conception of Mary. "In Her occurs the miracle of the union of God with creation." From the moment of the Incarnation, "the Father through the Son and the Holy Spirit infuses no supernatural life into the soul, except through the Mediatrix of all grace, the Immaculate" (*SK* III, 1310, p. 721). Thus, divine life, the life of love of the most Blessed Trinity "flows from the Sacred Heart of Jesus through the Immaculate Heart of Mary into our poor hearts" (*SK* I, 503, p. 920). "And similarly, the love of creatures reaches Jesus through Her, and through Jesus, the Father." Our acts of love "in the Immaculate acquire an immaculate purity, whereas in Jesus they acquire infinite value" so as to honor the most Blessed Trinity worthily. "Creatures are not always aware of this; nonetheless, this is how it always occurs" (*SK* III, 1310, pp. 721ff.), by the gracious disposition of God.

In practice, we accept this entire economy of God by consecrating ourselves totally to the Immaculate, as Her property, for our entire life and eternity. And, at times, we renew this consecration in special circumstances, offering her our individual works, our acts of devotion, including the eucharistic.

> Anyone consecrated to the Immaculate totally and without restriction, whenever he makes a visit to Jesus in the Blessed Sacrament, quite apart from his awareness of belonging to Her (to which he may not always advert), will offer the entire visit expressly to the Immaculate, even if only with the invocation "Mary", because he knows this will bring the maximum joy possible to Jesus and because he realizes also that in this instance it is She who accomplishes that visit in him and through him and he in Her and through Her. So, too, there is no better preparation for Holy Communion than to offer it all to the Immaculate (naturally doing on our part all that we can). She will prepare our heart in the best way possible, and we can be certain to bring Jesus the greatest joy possible and to show Him the greatest love (*SK* II, 643, p. 206).

With this in mind, Father Kolbe, when in Japan he was informed that plans were being made to erect a church at Niepokalanów, immediately submitted this design:

> At the high altar I would like to see a beautiful statue of the Immaculate with arms outstretched, forming a backdrop for the monstrance during perpetual adoration of the Blessed Sacrament as the brothers take their turns at adoration. Whoever should make a visit to the chapel—"Basilica"—would kneel, remain in adoration [of the Blessed Sacrament], glance at the Immaculate and depart, leaving Her with Jesus to resolve his problem. So, too, She handles the affairs of the missions, the hard, stony hearts of the pagans. Above the statue, in the window [of the wall], a beautiful representation of the Heart of Jesus (*SK* II, 585, p. 99).

In this matter, however, Father Kolbe encountered objections. Even his brother, Father Alphonse, caricaturing his thought, complained: "Why always, literally always, this: 'Come only to Mary, and if to Jesus, then with Her?' The days of the Old Testament are gone and God is accessible today! 'Come to me all' is the invitation. Why block the way to the Lord Jesus?" (Alph., pp. 265ff.). Once, in Japan, Father Maximilian received a letter from Brother Matthew Spolitakiewicz in Niepokalanów, wherein he articulated his difficulties. He wrote:

> I have not succeeded in harmonizing in my soul the fact of loving at the same moment Jesus and Mary. I go before the tabernacle. I engage in conversation with Jesus. . . . Where, then, is Mary, without whom it is difficult to approach Jesus . . . ? Or can I speak directly with Jesus without thinking

of Mary . . . ? She must certainly receive something from me, I must breathe of Her, live of Her. . . . But, but Jesus is properly the source of grace and love. He calls to Himself, He gives Himself in Holy Communion. In this Mary is only a help (*SK* II, 643, pp. 202ff.).

Father Maximilian answered with patience and clarity. He explained to that scrupulous brother that his difficulties arose from his confusing feeling, memory, intellect, and will. As regards love, we can and must love all together, simultaneously, "only we cannot think of all in the same moment." But this is no impediment to that love. "It is not only 'difficult'," he corrected, "but impossible to approach Jesus without Mary", since it is the will of God that "all graces come to us passing through Her, in the same way as Jesus himself came in our midst through Her." But in affirming this, it does not follow that we must feel, remember, and understand the intercession of Mary, either generally or in particular cases. It is enough to believe it.

> If you truly love Jesus, then first of all you desire to do His will, and hence to receive grace in the manner ordained by Him. If you have such a disposition, then you can quite freely, indeed you should turn to the Sacred Heart of Jesus with the conviction you will obtain everything. But if someone should say to himself: "I do not need anyone's mediation, I have no need of Mary most holy, I am on my own in condition to adore and do homage to the Sacred Heart of Jesus and to ask Him for whatever I need", would not Jesus have reason to

reject him for such insufferable pride? (*SK* II, 643, pp. 202ff.).

The saint repeated incessantly that with Mary, consecrated to her, even when not thinking of her, or invoking her expressly, we go to Jesus most quickly, because she has removed the obstacles, leaving us to advance in greater confidence and freedom (cf. *CK*, June 26, 1936; December 31, 1938).

> A soul consecrated to the Immaculate should follow in full freedom the inclination of his heart and draw closer with greater confidence both to the Tabernacle and to the Cross, and to the most Blessed Trinity, for such a soul does not approach alone, but together with his heavenly Mother, the Immaculate. Such a soul, then, should pray freely, whether with ejaculations, or with other prayers, because she is lifted aloft on the wings of divine love, wherever the Holy Spirit breathes, breaking every barrier (*SK* III, 1301, p. 706).

In all this is clearly evident the formative action of the Immaculate and the efficacy of her grace, facilitated by our unlimited consecration. The more we are likened to the Immaculate, the more we will love her Son. "I wish you"—and this greeting of Father Kolbe to his confreres in Japan can be addressed to all members of the MI—

> to draw closer every day, every moment to the Immaculate, to know Her ever more perfectly, to love Her always more, to allow yourselves to be permeated ever more deeply by Her thoughts, Her sentiments, Her intentions, Her love for the Child

Jesus in the crib, in the house at Nazareth, on the Cross, in the Eucharist and in Paradise; in a word I wish you to become ever more like the Immaculate and become always more—like Her—immaculate (SK II, 757, pp. 360–61).

On the occasion of the solemnity of the Immaculate Conception, it is the custom for members of the MI to make an examination of conscience covering the past year to see whether, through the Immaculate, they have drawn closer to the Sacred Heart of Jesus, conversed in greater familiarity with Jesus in the tabernacle and even more after having received Him in holy Communion (SK III, 1233, p. 543). On that solemn day, deeply conscious of our ideals and of our choice of life, "we beseech"—as the saint encourages us—"the Immaculate to prepare our hearts to receive Her divine Son worthily", and after holy Communion, "we beseech the Immaculate again that She herself keep company with Jesus in our souls and make Him happy as no one else has so far succeeded in doing. We beseech Her to offer to Jesus fitting reparation, both for our infidelities and for the many insults He every day endures throughout the world from sinners" (SK III, 1234, p. 545). A better fine-tuning of heart and soul for the entire year could not be found.

After having addressed in such wise the souls of the Militia of the Immaculate, particularly those of the members at Niepokalanów and his own, Father Kolbe could on various occasions give special directives, at times underscoring the Marian dimension of the spiritual life, at others the eucharistic. It is worth examining at least one such directive on how to conduct ourselves during the visit to the Prisoner of love. "If time permits," he said to his brothers at Niepokalanów,

> and should we be free of duty or passing near the chapel, let us not forget to visit our Prisoner, if only for a minute; this will be pleasing to Jesus. Let us tell Him we love Him. We might ask Him what He wants of us, what are His wishes. Sometimes we might ask Jesus something for ourselves and something for others. One can speak to Jesus as brother to brother, as friend to friend, more so, since it often happens that men do not understand us, whereas Jesus understands each of us always. Such conversations are pleasing to Jesus.

Brother Swietoslaus Jarkowski, recounting this encouragement of the saint, adds: "From these words it is evident that he himself spoke to Jesus with such confidence" (*Dok.* II, 1, p. 95).

Without doubt, his faith and love are shown still more in the practice of virtue, in the common life of the brotherhood, in a zealous apostolate, in habitual readiness for sacrifice. He also reminded others that our love for God cannot stop at enthusiasm during prayer, in fact not always possible, even near the altar, because of our nature, but must express itself in a life of sacrifice. Eucharistic and Marian devotion must lead us to such a life. In 1933 Father Kolbe wrote from Shanghai to the missionaries at Mugenzai no Sono:

> Dear sons, let us remember that love lives, is nourished by sacrifices. Let us thank the Immaculate for

interior peace, for the ecstasies of love. Let us not forget that all this, though good and inspiring, is not the essential of love. Indeed love, even perfect love, can exist without all this. [Rather], . . . without sacrifice there is no love. The sacrifice of the senses . . . but above all the sacrifice of reason and of will in holy obedience. When the love of the Immaculate, of the goodness of God in Her, of the love of the Divine Heart personified in Her, when such love will have pierced and permeated us, then sacrifices will become a necessity for our souls (*SK* I, 503, p. 922).

There is no doubt Saint Maximilian learned this lesson at the foot of the altar and there found continual stimulus and the strength to return the love of Jesus with a love ready for any sacrifice, for the hardest tasks in the cause of His Sacred Heart, through the Immaculate. After each visit, he left the friary chapel with a stronger faith and hope, with a heart more aflame with love, with tireless zeal. "Before the Divine Prisoner of love," reflected Brother Luke Kuzba, observing his superior in adoration, "his heart opened in limitless love and by means of His strength there strengthened his faith. I thought him to be a true knight of the Immaculate, the model of the MI. And seeing how radiant was his face, I was convinced that, had he been required at that moment to give his life for the Faith, he would have done so without hesitation" (*Dok.* II, 1, p. 143). This he did in the hour indicated by the Lord, through the strength of the grace implored at the foot of the altar.

The World: One Family through the Eucharist

The devotion of Saint Maximilian to the most Blessed Sacrament was commemorated at the 37th International Eucharistic Congress "Pro Mundi Vita", held in 1960 in Munich, Germany. On August 3, the day reserved for the MI, Father Agathon Kandler, O.F.M. Conv., spoke on the "eucharistic life of the Militia of the Immaculate". Archbishop Nicholas Canino, a member of the MI, celebrated Mass for the movement, stressing in his homily how "Father Kolbe, after the example of Jesus, gave his life for a brother, inviting us to follow his example in conquering all our brothers for Christ through the Immaculate." Cardinal Julius Döpfner, addressing all the participants assembled in the great plaza of the congress, proposed the Martyr of Charity as an example to be imitated. "Only with men such as Father Kolbe," he said, "who live their Christianity integrally, can we today approach and guide a lost mankind to the house of the Father, and thus to salvation" (*L'Immacolata e il suo Cuore* [September 1960]: 2).

Saint Maximilian wished to lead all men to the house of the Father, i.e., to the Church, and thus to make them happy, first on earth and then fully in eternity. And, as a means, he used, above all, that love ready for every sacrifice on behalf of all, a love enkindled and fed at the altar, continually formed by the Immaculate. For the Militia of the Immaculate, he outlined the same ideal: "To conquer hearts for the Immaculate with love and through Her for the divine Heart of Jesus and ultimately for the heavenly Father" (*SK* III, 1237, p. 549). This is, as we have seen, the response to the salvific work of Christ, the work of love. "To attract souls", wrote Father Kolbe during the war, "and transform them into Himself through love, Christ has revealed His own infinite love, His own Heart inflamed by love for souls, a love that impelled Him to mount the Cross, to remain with us in the Eucharist, and to enter our souls and to leave us in testament His own Mother as our Mother" (*SK* III, 1296, p. 699).

Christ instituted the Eucharist out of love and for love, to set our hearts aflame with the love of God and of neighbor. On Holy Thursday, Father Kolbe usually reminded the friars of Niepokalanów "of those last moments following on the institution of the Blessed Sacrament" and referred to Saint John the Evangelist who "better than anyone understood the Heart of the Lord Jesus." He would read chapter 13 and the subsequent chapters of his Gospel, making brief comments.

> Let us see how important it was to Jesus that His disciples be one, after the example of the unity between Him and His Father, so that they might love each other, and thus the world might come to know that they were His disciples. Jesus had us as well in mind at that time; thus, we must be diligent in practicing mutual charity within common life. ... Mutual charity consists in serving each other and in bearing one another's burdens, at one's own expense (*CK*, March 25, 1937).

He himself, aspiring to the greatest love possible, took to heart these words of the Savior: "Greater love than this no one has, that one lay down his life for his friends" (Jn 15:13), words quoted in an article entitled "The Religion of Love" in *Seibo no Kishi*, which began with the words:

> Hate divides, separates, and destroys, whereas, on the contrary, love unites, gives peace, builds up. It is not strange, therefore, that only love should always be able to make men perfect. Hence, only that religion which teaches the love of God and of neighbor can perfect men. The religion of Jesus Christ is truly this religion of perfect love and that is evident in the holy words of Jesus Christ.

After having quoted many statements of Jesus about love, Father Kolbe concluded the article in this way: "It is fair to assert that, were this religion spread throughout the world, the world would become paradise" (*SK* III, 1205, pp. 464, 466).

Earlier, during his youth, reflecting on the instructions given by Jesus at the Last Supper and on the Cross, the saint observed: "Jesus Himself gave Himself to you and has given you His Mother.... Ask: 1) love for Him, since He has loved you as much as the Father has loved Him ... [and] 2) to love one's neighbor as He has loved you" (*SK* II, 962, p. 617). On the last day of 1917, the year of the founding of the MI, he resolved: "Love! This is everything" (*SK* II, 987 A, p. 680). Father Kolbe was convinced that "the love of God is the only source of authentic and sincere love of neighbor" (*SK* III, 1093, p. 209).

"Authentic love lifts one above the created and immerses one in God: in Him and through Him and by means of Him love all, good and bad, friends and enemies. To all extend a hand full of love, pray for all, suffer for all, wish well to all, desire happiness for all, since it is God who wills it!" (*SK* III, 1075, p. 161). The closer we draw to God, the closer we draw to each other. The Eucharist is precisely the "sign of unity, bond of charity", as the Church teaches (Vatican II, *Sacrosanctum concilium*, no. 47).

Christ not only gives His "new commandment" of love, but also, with His grace, makes man able to observe this commandment. Father Kolbe made his own a prayer of Saint Thérèse of the Child Jesus, which he probably brought, in his own words or wordlessly, before the altar during adoration. Here is the text of this prayer, quoted by him in one of his letters as a model for others as well:

> My sweet Jesus, I know that you do not command anything impossible, you know better than I my weaknesses, my imperfections. You know well that I will not succeed even in loving my sisters as you love them, if you yourself do not love in me and through me. This is why you grant me this grace, who gave me your new commandment. Oh, how I love your commandment, for it gives the assurance that you wish to love through me all whom you have commanded me to love.

After citing these words, he added: "The profounder this love, the more efficacious will missionary activity be" (*SK* II, 925, p. 566), no doubt remembering as well the example of Saint Thérèse, who, in loving thus, became the patroness of the missions. And so much the more does forgiveness of wrongs done us aid that cause, in accord with the Our Father: "Forgive us our trespasses as we forgive those who trespass against us." We recite this prayer just before Communion, hoping to find in it the necessary courage.

Saint Maximilian worked hard to establish in the name of the eucharistic Jesus and of the Immaculate an authentically fraternal spirit in his Niepokalanów. Every city of the Immaculate is, and must be, one single family governed by the law of love, thus becoming a sign for others. Father Kolbe reflected with pleasure:

> Niepokalanów is the cottage at Nazareth. God the Father is Father, the Immaculate is Mother and mistress of the house, Jesus in the Blessed Sacrament of the altar the only-begotten Son and our Brother. All the younger brothers, for their part, strive to imitate the elder Brother in loving and honoring God and the Immaculate, our common parents; from the Immaculate they learn to love their divine elder Brother, their main example, their ideal of holiness, who deigned to come down from heaven, to become incarnate in Her and to take up His abode in our midst in the tabernacle (*SK* III, 1284, p. 681).

It is no surprise that "all the rest are not comrades, but brothers, younger brothers, that is, who love each other" (*SK* III, 1222, p. 498).

The cities of the Immaculate, as MI centers, have an apostolic goal. "Our task", Father Kolbe recalled during the war, "is the transformation of the world, of men, of souls in the Immaculate" (*CK*, April 7, 1940). But it is their interior development, their progress in charity that is the essential thing. "The MI center, to be truly such, must itself be ablaze, to be capable of radiating beyond itself, just as does the sun which brightens, warms, and vivifies." So too, should the friars be dispersed on account of persecution, "the sparks spread abroad, namely, their hearts, would ignite new flames about them, and thus the scope of Niepokalanów would be achieved" (*CK*, March 8, 1940). Such also is the commitment of every member of the MI. As a movement, the MI grows in virtue of its inner power, through the dynamism of love in each of its members; it acts with a zeal reminiscent of the first Christians, often drawing close to the altar, always as an instrument of the Immaculate.

With his pen, or rather with his heart, Saint Maximilian, at times, wrote passages ablaze with zeal. For example, in 1933, for the first Sunday after Easter, he wrote aboard ship:

> Where the scope of the MI is achieved, as soon as possible, that is, when the conquest for the Immaculate of the whole world and of every single soul now living or to live until the end of the world, and through Her for the Most Sacred Heart of Jesus is completed, . . . then souls will love the Sacred Heart as they have never as yet loved Him, because like Her they will have been immersed as never before in the mystery of love: the Cross, the Eucharist. Through Her the love of God will inflame the

world, will set it on fire, and will effect the "assumption" of souls, . . . the divinization of the entire world (SK II, 991 Q, p. 895).

The founder of the MI was convinced, as he declared, on December 8, 1937, on Polish National Radio in a broadcast to all Poland, that

when the spirit of Niepokalanów, the spirit of the MI, penetrates our country and the entire world, when the Immaculate will have become Queen of every heart beating under the sun, then paradise will come on earth, not the paradise of communists and socialists, but—in so far as it is possible on earth—the true paradise. The happiness of this paradise at this moment is the joy of those who dwell at Niepokalanów, where there is but one family, of which God is the Father, the Immaculate is the Mother, the Divine Prisoner of love in the Eucharist the elder Brother, while all the rest are not merely comrades, but younger brothers who love each other (SK III, 1222, p. 498; cf. CK, November 8, 1936).

But are we not moving in a realm of dreams and pious desires? The saint, ever aiming for the best (he was called a "man of desires"—cf. Dan 9:23), implemented his stupendous plans in a practical way, beginning with himself, with individual souls, and families. Full of joy, even in the midst of tribulations (cf. his confidences made January 10, 1937, Dok. II, 1, p. 157), he suggested that everyone, after a good confession, should seek "to receive Jesus in the Eucharist and never allow his soul to remain in sin, . . . do good to all, including one's enemies, solely for the love of God . . . then would he realize what is meant by a foretaste of paradise . . ." (*SK* III, 1065, p. 146). In the peace of his own family, close to the Mother of God, he experienced what it means to live the Eucharist under the mantle of the Mother of God. Father Kolbe encouraged the readers of *Rycerz* thus:

> People of little faith, why does doubt stealthily slip into your heart? Enkindle everywhere love for and confidence in the Immaculate, and very soon you will see tears of repentance well up in the eyes of the most obdurate sinners, the prisons emptied, the ranks of honest laborers swelled, while domestic hearths will radiate the fragrance of virtue; peace and happiness will erase discord and sadness, because a new era has dawned (*SK* III, 1069, p. 153).

Notwithstanding communist propaganda over many years, the churches in Poland are still full [this study was written in 1982, before the fall of the communist regime in Poland—TRANS.], a phenomenon due in great part to Saint Maximilian and his Niepokalanów, which gives strength to the nation to endure its lot. And the final sacrifice of the saint in giving his own life to save that of a father of a family condemned to death in the concentration camp of Oświęcim "is a challenge to our contemporaries, to the nations and to society; he has become an eloquent sign for the times in which we live", as Pope John Paul II remarked (*OR* [August 27, 1982]: 2). Thus one advances toward final victory.

The full realization of the ideal of the MI will occur in paradise where, according to Father Kolbe, "there is also a Niepokalanów, since there too are the same Father, the same Mother and the same elder Brother with His body" (*SK* III, 1284, p. 682), no longer veiled under the eucharistic species. In heaven, love and joy without measure and without end will fully reign. "How grateful to us", the founder told the members of the MI, "will be those countless legions of souls to whom we opened the gates of heaven. . . . What a hymn of adoration, of glory and of thanks will rise from all the citizens of heaven to the Heart of Jesus for having given us so kind a Mother", the Immaculate. "And thus, all of us, together with the Immaculate, will thank and adore forever the mercy, the goodness, the wisdom, the power and the justice of God, in possessing the reward which He promised us" (*SK* III, 1248, pp. 583ff.).

Afterword

Perhaps one may be surprised that Saint Maximilian, loving Jesus so ardently, one of the most zealous adorers of the most Blessed Sacrament, spoke and wrote so much more about the Immaculate, and when teaching about Christ, hardly ever omitted His Mother. Without doubt, he respected the hierarchy of truths, always placing first the most Blessed Trinity and Jesus Christ, our Lord. But once recognizing the masterpiece of God—the Immaculate—after discovering her role in the divine economy of salvation, and in seeking to increase the love of God and of neighbor on earth, he felt called to make more accessible her goodness and power and to unite everyone with her in the most perfect way possible. He realized that thus he could lead men most easily to Christ and render to God the greatest glory possible. Such was his prophetic mission, as Pope John Paul II said June 18, 1983, at Niepokalanów. He added at Jasna Góra that Saint Maximilian clears a path for the Church in our difficult 20th century.

On the Feast of Saint Maximilian, priest and martyr, the Church commands us to pray, during the Mass in his honor, in this fashion after Communion: "Having received Your Body and Your Blood we beseech You, Lord Jesus: may the fire of charity which Saint Maximilian Mary drew from this Sacred Banquet enkindle our hearts as well." This prayer is an official homage of the Church to this priest and a guide for all his devotees.

ABBREVIATIONS

Alph. Alphonse Kolbe, O.F.M. Conv. *Notatki* (Notes), vol. 5. 1928–1929. Manuscript.

BMK *Beatyfikacja Ojca Maksymiliana Marii Kolbe. Wybór dokumentów i przemówien* (The beatification of Fr. Maximilian M. Kolbe. Select documents and discourses). Rome: Gregorian University Press, 1971.

CK *Konferencja ascetyczne. Notatki słuchaczy przemówien Ojca Maksymiliana Kolbego* (Ascetical conferences of Fr. Maximilian Kolbe from the notes of those who heard him). Niepokalanów, 1976. (After the abbreviation the date of the conference is indicated.)

Dok. *Dokumenty o Ojca Maksymilianie M. Kolbem* (Documents concerning Fr. Maximilian M. Kolbe). Vol. I: *Oswiadczneia osób spoza Zakonu franciszkanskiego* (Declarations of persons outside the Franciscan Order). Niepokalanów, 1958. Vol. II: *Oswiadczenia wspólbraci zakonnych* (Declarations of confreres). Part 1, Niepokanalów, 1953. Part 2, Niepokalanów, 1979. Typescript.

HD	*Homo Dei* (Polish clerical journal) 40, no. 4 (1971) (dedicated to Blessed Maximilian Kolbe).
L	*Błogosławiony Maksymilian wsród nas* (Blessed Maximilian among us). Warsaw: Ed. SS. Loretanki, 1972.
LP	*Litterae Postulatoriae*. In *Positio super introductione causae* (Postulatory letters, in deposition for the introduction of the cause). Part 6. Rome, 1957.
M	*Błogosławiony Maksymilian Maria Kolbe. Dokumenty, artykuły, opracowania* (Blessed Maximilian Mary Kolbe. Documents, articles, commentaries). Niepokalanów, 1974.
Miles	*Miles Immaculatae* (Roman scholarly journal).
OR	*L'Osservatore Romano* (Vatican daily).
P	Karol Wojtyła (Pope John Paul II), *Massimiliano Kolbe. Patrono del nostro difficile secolo* (Maximilian Kolbe: patron of our troubled century). Vatican City: Vatican Press, 1982.
Pisma	*Pisma Ojca Maksymiliana Marii Kolbego Franciszkanina* (Writings of Fr. Maximilian M. Kolbe). Vols. I–VII. Niepokalanów, 1970. Mimeograph (original edition of the writings).

Pos.   *Beatificationis et canonizationis Servi Dei Maximiliani M. Kolbe . . . Positio super virtutibus* (Deposition on the virtues . . . for the beatification and canonization of the Servant of God Maximilian M. Kolbe). Rome, 1966.

Rel.   *Relacje osób duchownych i swieckich o Ojcu Maksymilianie Kolbem* (Accounts of Fr. Maximilian Kolbe by religious and laypeople). Niepokalanów, 1969. Typescript.

RN   *Rycerz Niepokalanej* (Knight of the Immaculate). (Polish monthly founded by St. Maximilian.)

SK   *Gli Scritti di Massimiliano Kolbe eroe di Oswiecim e beato della Chiesa* (The writings of Maximilian Kolbe, hero of Oświęcim and blessed of the Church). Vols. I–III. Florence: Città di Vita, 1975–1978. (Italian translation of the writings of the saint: cited by volume, article number, page.)

Zez.   *Zeznania wspólwiezniów* (Depositions of fellow prisoners). Niepokalanów, 1970. Typescript.

An English translation of all the known writings and conferences of Saint Maximilian is in preparation. When it appears, citations in this book from these works will be able to be located easily via either the standard number of each writing or the date of each conference.